ARABIC   ASTRONOMY   BANKING   BEE-KEEPING   BIOLOGY
GANISATION   CALCULUS   CANASTA   CARPENTRY   CHEMISTRY
COMMERCIAL CORRESPONDENCE   COMMERCIAL TRAVELLING   TO
OKING   CRICKET   DRAWING   DRE   DUTTON
ELECTRICITY IN THE   BROIDERY
ENGLISH RENASCENCE   OMANTIC
EVERYDAY FRENCH   TO   TO FLY
ASE BOOK   GARDENING   APHY OF
IONARY   GERMAN GRA   GOLF
GOOD FARM ACCOUNTING   FARMING
UIT FARMING   GOOD GRA   AND HEALTHY ANIMALS
GOOD POULTRY KEEPING   GOOD SHEEP FARMING   GOOD SOIL
LE   HINDUSTANI   HISTORY: ABRAHAM LINCOLN ALEXANDER THE
EAU   CONSTANTINE   COOK   CRANMER   ERASMUS   GLADSTONE AND
MILTON   PERICLES   PETER THE GREAT   PUSHKIN   RALEIGH   RICHELIEU
OODROW   EMENT
ALIAN   LETTER
ENGIN   ANICS
ODERN   ···· AND HE WILL BE   ORING
PHILOSO   HYSICS
PLUMBI   YET WISER Proverbs 9.9   PUBLIC
RECKO   USSIAN
X: ITS N   AND PURPOSE   SOCCER   SPANISH   SPE   AND
SWA   SWEDISH   TEACHING   THINKING   TRIG   METRY
BRI H RAILWAYS FOR BOYS   CAMPING FOR BOYS AND GIRLS
FOR GIRLS   MODELMAKING FOR BOYS   NEEDLEWORK FOR GIRLS
BOYS AND GIRLS   SAILING AND SMALL BOATS FOR BOYS AND GIRLS
VORK FOR BOYS   ADVERTISING & PUBLICITY   ALGEBRA   AMATEUR
PING   BIOLOGY   BOOK-KEEPING   BRICKWORK   BRINGING UP
ENTRY   CHEMISTRY   CHESS   CHINESE   COMMERCIAL ARITHMETIC
TRAVELLING   TO COMPOSE MUSIC   CONSTRUCTIONAL DETAILS
NG   DUTCH   DUTTON SPEEDWORDS   ECONOMIC GEOGRAPHY
IST   EMBROIDERY   ENGLISH GRAMMAR   LITERARY APPRECIATION
VIVAL   ROMANTIC REVIVAL   VICTORIAN AGE   CONTEMPORARY
FISHING   TO FLY   FREELANCE WRITING   FRENCH   FRENCH
OUSE   GEOGRAPHY OF LIVING THINGS   GEOLOGY   GEOMETRY
RASE BOOK   GOLF   GOOD CONTROL OF INSECT PESTS   GOOD
FARM CROPS   GOOD FARMING   GOOD FARMING BY MACHINE
ND   GOOD AND HEALTHY ANIMALS   GOOD MARKET GARDENING
GOOD SHEEP FARMING   GOOD SOIL   GOOD ENGLISH   GREEK
TORY ABRAHAM LINCOLN   ALEXANDER THE GREAT   BOLIVAR   BOTHA
CRANMER ERASMUS GLADSTONE AND LIBERALISM   HENRY V   JOAN OF
REAT PUSHKIN RALEIGH RICHELIEU ROBESPIERRE THOMAS JEFFERSON
HOME NURSING   HORSE MANAGEMENT   HOUSEHOLD DOCTOR
OURNALISM   LATIN   LAWN TENNIS   LETTER WRITER   MALAY
PONENTS   WORKSHOP PRACTICE   MECHANICS   MECHANICAL
G   MORE GERMAN   MOTHERCRAFT   MOTORING   MOTOR CYCLING
RAPHY   PHYSICAL GEOGRAPHY   PHYSICS   PHYSIOLOGY   PITMAN'S
GUESE   PSYCHOLOGY   PUBLIC ADMINISTRATION   PUBLIC SPEAKING

THE TEACH YOURSELF BOOKS
EDITED BY LEONARD CUTTS

CONTRACT BRIDGE

**Uniform with this volume
and in the same
series**

Teach Yourself Amateur Acting
Teach Yourself Athletics
Teach Yourself Billiards and Snooker
Teach Yourself Canasta
Teach Yourself Card Games for Two
Teach Yourself Chess
Teach Yourself Conjuring
Teach Yourself Cricket
Teach Yourself Cycling
Teach Yourself Fishing
Teach Yourself Golf
Teach Yourself Hockey
Teach Yourself Judo
Teach Yourself Lawn Tennis
Teach Yourself Motoring
Teach Yourself Motor Boating
Teach Yourself Motor Cycling
Teach Yourself Rugby Football
Teach Yourself Sailing
Teach Yourself Soccer
Teach Yourself Stamp Collecting
Teach Yourself Swimming

TEACH YOURSELF

CONTRACT BRIDGE

By
J. G. HARTLEY

THE ENGLISH UNIVERSITIES PRESS LTD
102 NEWGATE STREET
LONDON, E.C.1

First printed . . . 1949
This impression . . 1957

Printed in Great Britain for the English Universities Press, Limited,
by C. Tinling & Co., Ltd., Liverpool, London and Prescot.

CONTENTS

DEFINITIONS

BID : An offer to contract to make a certain number of tricks in a specified denomination.

CONTRACT : The last bid in the auction.

DECLARER : The player who for his side first bids the denomination named in the contract.

DEFENDER : During the auction a member of the side which does not open the bidding After the bidding has ended, an opponent of the declarer.

DOUBLETON : An original holding of only two cards of a suit.

DUMMY : Declarer's partner whose cards are placed face upwards on the table after the first card has been led.

FORCING BID: A bid which compels the partner to bid. Some of the bids are forcing for one round, others are forcing until game is reached.

GAME : A trick score of 100 points.

GRAND SLAM FORCE : A bid which asks the partner to bid seven of the agreed suit if he holds two of the three top honours.

HONOUR CARD : The ace, king, queen, knave or ten of a suit.

HONOUR TRICK : A trick taken by an honour card.

OVER-TRICK : A trick won by the declarer in excess of his contract.

REVOKE : The play of a card of another suit when able to follow suit.

RUBBER : Two games won by one side.

RUFF : To trump a side suit.

SINGLETON : An original holding of only one card in a suit.

SLAM : A contract to make 12 or 13 tricks. A contract to make 12 tricks is a small slam, and to make 13 tricks a grand slam.

SYSTEM : The system of bidding employed by a partnership. Only recognized systems may be used.

TAKE OUT : The bid of another suit after a bid by partner.

TENACE : Two cards not in sequence which if led up to may make two tricks but if led out may make only one. The ace and queen of a suit are a major tenace.

TRUMP : Each card of the suit named in the contract.

UNDER-TRICK : A trick by which the declarer falls short of his contract.

VOID : An original holding of no card in a suit.

VULNERABLE : A side becomes vulnerable when it has made one game.

YARBOROUGH : A hand which contains no card higher than a nine.

I

CONTRACT BRIDGE

BRIDGE is a game. What is more it is a good game, one of the most popular ever invented, and it is played by millions of people throughout the world. But it is more than a game, it is also a social asset. A good Bridge player finds a ready welcome in many social circles which would be closed to him or her without the ability to play the game with a certain amount of skill. One of the great changes which the world has seen in the last fifty years has been in the social occupations of the people. In the days of Queen Victoria musical evenings and afternoon at-homes brought together the friends who sought entertainment and pleasure in their leisure hours. To-day, afternoon and evening Bridge parties have taken their place and the issue of invitations is determined not so much by the personality of those to whom they are sent as by knowledge of and ability to play the game. A good player can find his entertainment in a very wide circle, a poor player, however charming his or her personality, has a very limited choice.

While proficiency at Bridge comes very largely by practice, the object of this book is to lay a foundation which will enable the reader to take his place at the bridge table and to hold his own in the company of players of average standard. There is no game at which it is more advisable to learn something of the elementary rules, though when we come down to fundamentals the two great foundations of successful play are common

A*

sense and the ability to count up to thirteen. Every bid that is made, every card that is played conveys information and the game does much to develop the reasoning and deductive powers of the players.

2

THE PACK

THERE are few people who have not handled a pack of
cards or who do not know that it consists of 52 cards
divided into four suits of 13 cards each. The origin of
playing cards is lost in antiquity. There have been
historians who asserted that they came originally from
China, from India, from Persia and from Egypt while
from America we have been told that playing cards were
in use in the time of Joseph but that they did not appear
among the Jews until after the return from the Baby-
lonian exile. It has also been asserted that they were
brought to Europe by the Crusaders but there is no
written evidence that they existed before the Fourteenth
century when many people declared they were the invention of the devil, a view which has received the ready
approval of some players after a session of bridge when
everything has gone wrong.

In the early days of card playing in this country there
was a determined effort to confine it to the upper classes.
It was held up as a distraction from the practice of
archery and a hindrance to the steady work of the common people. But its popularity increased steadily and
in the days of Queen Elizabeth an import ban was im-
posed to protect our card making industry, while Charles
the First found in a duty on playing cards a considerable
source of revenue for himself and his successors. While
the number of card players increased steadily with the
centuries, it was not until Bridge was invented that card

playing reached its zenith. By 1939 there were many millions of bridge players, and during the war many more millions were added to their number. Bridge was one of the sources of recreation for our Fighting Services and Civil Defence Forces and very often the first question put to a new-comer was not what did he know about his work but did he play Bridge.

Coming back to the pack with which the game is played, the four suits into which it is divided have definite values, spades ranking highest followed by hearts, diamonds and clubs. Spades and hearts are described as major suits and diamonds and clubs as minor suits. In the auction to decide in what contract the deal shall be played a bid of the same number of tricks in a higher ranking suit takes preference. The thirteen cards in the suit are in order of importance, ace, king, queen, knave, ten, nine, eight, seven, six, five, four, three, two. The knave is frequently described as the jack, the two as the deuce, and the nine of diamonds as the Curse of Scotland.

Though there are only 52 cards which are dealt in rotation to the four players the possible ways in which these cards may be divided staggers the imagination. An expert mathematician has put the figure at approximately 1,000,000,000,000,000,000,000,000,000,000, different ways. Other experts take exception to approximations and demand the exact figures but after all 1,000,000,000,000,000,000,000,000,000,000, is a nice handy figure, easy to remember, and a few millions or thousands of millions make little difference when the total is so large that it baffles human imagination to realize what it means. Curiously enough, though the odds against it are so tremendous, in a duplicate competition, a few years ago, identical hands were dealt to the competitors at two of the tables.

Even more remarkable was a deal in a game of rubber Bridge in London in 1943. South dealt and bid One Diamond, West bid Three Diamonds and North passed. East now bid Six Diamonds. When this bid was doubled by North, East redoubled. The play started and it was quickly discovered that there was something wrong with the pack. The cards were tabled and the amused players found the explanation of the curious bidding. There were two complete suits of diamonds and no hearts. It was a new pack and this was the first deal of the evening. West and North each held seven diamonds, while East and South had six each, but none of the players had two diamonds of the same value. And there are players in London today who are still waiting expectantly the arrival of a pack of cards with two complete suits of hearts and no diamonds.

Mathematical odds while extremely useful to show the normal expectancy in the division of the cards should not be taken too seriously by the bridge player. They are based on the assumption that there is always a perfect shuffle of the pack and this is far from being the case. The dealing of the cards, the collection of four cards of a suit in a trick, the play of a high card on another high card in taking a trick, or of three low cards of a suit on a master card which is led, all affect the distribution of the cards in the next deal.

Bridge is a game for four players, North and South playing as partners against East and West. For the selection of players, if more than four wish to take part, and of partners, a pack of cards is spread face downwards on the table and each of those desiring to play draws a card. The two players drawing the highest ranking cards play as partners against the two players drawing the next high ranking cards. The ace ranks as the highest card and if cards of the same rank are drawn the value of the suit determines precedence. Although the mathematical odds against it are tremendous, the writer was one of four players forming a table, when the first three selected in turn the aces of spades, hearts and diamonds. They called to the fourth member of the party, who was looking out of the window, to cut the ace of clubs—and the ace of clubs duly appeared. These four players had previously formed a part of a party of nine cutting to form two tables on a railway journey. One of them, cutting first, turned up the queen of spades and remarked cheerfully, " I am in " but he was not, for the eight other members of the party turned up the four aces and four kings.

The player who draws the highest card when cutting for partners has the choice of seats and cards. As a general rule it makes little difference which seat he chooses but there are many superstitious players who note carefully the run of the cards and if it appears to have favoured the North-South or East-West positions, are guided in their choice by their deduction as to which are the lucky seats. More often than not it makes little difference which seats they chose, but there are times when for a whole evening the run of the good cards is consistently in one direction or there appears to be a hoodoo on one particular seat and these are hailed by the superstitious as confirmation of their belief. The superstitious, however, have the support of no less an authority than Mr. Ely Culbertson, who has told us " The derided Bridge players who insist on taking winning seats and playing with a particular deck of cards, and who are therefore accused of playing with their *derrieres* rather than with their heads, are probably more right than all the mathematicians. I am among the ' superstitious ' ones and to the question whether I change my seat and cards after losing several rubbers, my answer is that I do not wait to lose several rubbers but after the very first lost rubber insist on drawing for a new deal and pray that I will draw the highest card so as to have the first choice. Apparently cards run in streaks much oftener than the mathematical probabilities would indicate. This may be due in part to the purely physical fact that the court cards have more paint on them and thus are apt to stick together more, as well as to the fact of the artificial pattern formation. It may follow that the run of cards is profoundly affected by the atmospheric conditions, and even by the cycle of spots on the sun . . . well, anyway, the possibilities, if humorous, are at least fascinating." Mr. Culbertson has at any rate had the courage of his convictions for he tells us that he has frequently called for new cards, and paid for them, in the hope of getting out of the rut of uninteresting hands into the type of hands which are more susceptible to skill.

The four players having settled in their seats the player who cut the highest card has to deal. Before he does so the player on his left must shuffle the pack and it is then passed to the player on the dealer's right to make the cut. This is done by lifting a portion from the top and placing it towards the dealer beside the bottom portion. The dealer them completes the cut by placing the bottom portion uppermost. The cards are then dealt in a clockwise direction one card at a time, to each player starting with the player on his left and ending with the dealer.

While the deal is in progress the dealer's partner shuffles the second pack and places it face downwards on his right. When the deal has been completed the four players pick up their cards and sort them into suits. They are now ready to take part in the auction which will decide in what contract the cards will be played and who will be the declarer.

At Whist which was the popular game for four players in this country until it was relegated to a very minor place by the invention of Bridge, the trump suit was fixed, but at Bridge the players bid to decide which shall be the trump suit and what the contract shall be. At Whist all four hands are hidden but at Bridge the cards held by the partner of the declarer are placed face upwards on the table after the opening lead and the holder of these cards described as Dummy becomes mainly a spectator while the hand is played.

At Contract Bridge, partners cannot score more points towards game than the value of the contract in which they have elected to play. The score sheet is divided into two columns for the points scored for and against. Half-way down a line is drawn and below this line are scored points which count towards game while above it are placed points made by surplus tricks, by holding four honours in the trump suit in one hand, penalties when the opponents fail to make their contract and bonuses for slams. There are five possible denominations in which the contract may be selected. In order of precedence they are No Trumps, Spades, Hearts, Diamonds, Clubs. The first six tricks scored by a partnership known as "the book", do not count towards the score and when a player bids One No Trump or One of a suit, he says he is prepared to make seven tricks or one over " the book."

To score a game a partnership must make 100 points below the line and two games must be made to win the rubber. When a game is made by either side a line is drawn on the bottom half of the score sheet below the points already made for tricks and both sides start the next game with a nil score, for points scored by the side which lost the first game are not carried forward. If one side wins the first two games it is awarded 700 points for the rubber but if each side win a game the points for winning the rubber are reduced to 500.

The highest score at Bridge is obtained from No Trump contracts in which 40 points are awarded for the first trick (over six) and 30 points for each subsequent trick. The score of 40 + 30 + 30 makes it possible to make a game in one hand with a contract of Three No Trumps, while with spades and hearts, where 30 points are awarded for each trick over six, it is necessary to bid four, and with diamonds and clubs which score 20 points for each trick it is necessary to bid five to secure game on one hand. No Trump contracts are therefore much more popular than contracts in a suit. Even if a player contracts to make only One No Trump he is better off with a score of 40 below the line than he would be by making a contract of one in a trump suit for he would now require to make two tricks in a major suit or three in a minor, while if he had scored only 30 points on the first hand he would have to bid and make an additional trick for game.

Scoring at No Trumps was the subject of one of the biggest mysteries of the war. Without any apparent reason letters came to this country from all parts of the world, the writer received hundreds, asking whether there had been any change in the Laws of Bridge altering the scoring from 40–30–30 for tricks, to 30–30–40. This new method of scoring it was stated had been adopted widely particularly in the Middle and Far East. Though they had tried to find out the grounds on which the change had been made the inquirers had been unsuccessful. The change, however, was important, for with a part score of 40 points for making a contract of One No Trump a contract of Two Spades, Two Hearts, Three Diamonds or Three Clubs made subsequently, would give a game score, while if only 30 points were awarded for a contract of One No Trump it would be necessary to bid three in a major suit or four in a minor to make the 70 additional points necessary for game. The life of a Bridge Correspondent became a misery, inquiries still continued to pour in despite repeated published denials and were still being received in 1948. The Great No Trump Mystery was solved eventually, and like so many other mysteries had a very simple explanation. The Secretary of the National Bridge Laws Commission of America served during the war with one of the most secret of the war services, and playing Bridge with high ranking military and Government officers, he inadvertently scored the first two tricks at No Trumps as 30 points each and the third at 40 points. Nobody dreamed of questioning the Secretary of the National Bridge Laws Commission of America. If he scored 30–30–40, then 30–30–40 it must be. And when Generals played with members of their staff they insisted on 30–30–40. Quickly the new scoring for No Trumps spread through the ranks and officers transferred from one field of service to another carried the new scoring with them. Modern invention which has given us rapid air transport gave a speedier and much more wide spread circulation to the Great No Trump Mystery than even to the two great myths—

Russian armies with snow on their boots passing through England, and the Angels of Mons—of the 1914–1918 war. Seldom in the field of human entertainment has a small slip by one man affected so many.

When the pack has been shuffled and dealt, each of the four players, has thirteen cards in front of him. They are picked up and sorted into suits with the cards in the order of importance in each suit. It is important to so hold the cards that they can be seen only by the player to whom they have been dealt. There are players who will insist on so holding their cards that some at least are visible to an opponent. By so doing they impose a foolish handicap on themselves, for they may expose to the declarer the position of key cards in the partnership hands and he can plan his play with certainty instead of having to guess at their position with a strong possibility that he will make a wrong guess. There are few players who will be prepared to take advantage of this foolish exposure of the hand by an opponent, but it has been known to happen. There is an old story of a smart young man who was playing in a contract of Three No Trumps and could see from his own hand and the cards on the table that he could make nine tricks before it was necessary to lose the lead. Instead of doing so, however, he put dummy in to lead a spade up to ace, king, queen, ten of the suit in his own hand. When the opponent on his right played a small card he finessed the ten. The player on his left produced the knave and ran off four tricks in clubs. When he was reproached afterwards by a partner who bitterly resented the manner in which a perfectly safe contract had been thrown away he was equally indignant. " The young woman on my left showed me her cards," he declared, " and seeing that she had not got the knave of spades I thought I might as well make an over-trick. When I finessed the ten she fished out the knave from behind the ten of hearts." He added with emphasis, " The next time I play against that young woman I shall count her cards." This however is not the kind of bridge that most of us would care to play and the player who exposes his cards can be a perfect nuisance to his opponents who have to adopt uncomfortable attitudes to avoid seeing them.

Returning to the hands which have been dealt and have still to be bid it is now time to consider how to bid.

To make an opening bid a player should have slightly better than an average hand. An average hand is one which would give two honour tricks to each player, but as there are honour cards which may take tricks but are not included in the honour count, in practice we find that in most deals the honour tricks work out at between eight and nine. The average hand may therefore be taken to contain two plus honour tricks. To open the bidding the honour strength of the hand should be above the average. Honour cards alone are not the only consideration. It is estimated that as a rule they take only eight of the thirteen tricks. The remainder are taken by trumps and the long cards of a suit. In estimating the trick taking possibilities of a hand therefore it is necessary to consider not only its honour strength but also its shape. If the cards in the pack are divided evenly each player will have four cards in one suit and three cards in each of the others. If there are no trumps and three rounds of his four card suit are taken, each player can expect to take a trick with the fourth card of his four card suit, provided that he has a card in one of the other suits which will enable him to take a trick to enable him to lead his long card.

Distribution plays so important a part in the valuation of a hand for bidding purposes that its trick taking influence should be understood thoroughly. Take first the trump suit. In the first instance this should be regarded as likely to produce one long card trick for every card above three. With five cards of the suit therefore a player before making an opening bid assumes that he will make two tricks plus the expectancy of honour tricks in the suit. If the suit is headed by the ace and the king this combination will usually produce at least four tricks in play, while if it is headed by the three top honours it will produce five tricks. This valuation is made on the assumption that the partner can support the trump suit. If when his turn to bid comes he denies the suit by bidding a suit of his own, it is necessary for the opener to re-value his hand. In support of his partner's trump suit he can no longer count on making the same number of tricks with the long cards of his own suit for they may be ruffed if the suit is attacked before the opponent's trumps are drawn, while the fact that his partner cannot support the suit makes it probable that even if trumps are drawn one of the opponents may have long cards in the suit which will beat his own.

There is a separate valuation for cards in a side suit. Here the probable value of the fourth card of a suit is only one half of a trick with each card beyond four valued as one trick. This valuation however depends upon partnership agreement upon trumps, for unless the partners are agreed upon the suit there is no certainty that the opponents trumps can be drawn to enable long cards in a side suit to be made.

There is a different valuation of the hand when making an opening bid and when responding to the partner's bid. This may seem complicated but it is only common sense. When making an opening bid a player knows that there are certain cards missing and until he has heard what his partner has to say in response to his bid, he must be prepared to find those cards held by his opponents, though he is entitled to expect that some at least will be held by his partner. When responding to a bid made by his partner however, a player has more knowledge of the situation. He knows that his partner has a hand which is better than the average. If his partner has bid One Spade, for example, he knows that he must have at least four cards of the suit. If it is a four card suit two at least of those four cards should be honour cards. His partner in making his opening bid has valued his trump honours on the assumption that the missing honour cards in the suit are held by the opponents. In his own hand he can see the king, queen, nine of the suit. These cards fill in blanks in his partner's hand. If the opener has ace, knave, and two other cards he will have estimated the trick value of the spade suit as two—one for the ace and one for the long card. By filling in the blanks his own king and queen ensure four tricks in the suit and therefore king and queen, though they count only as one honour trick, actually add two tricks to the probable trick value. He will therefore, in valuing the probable tricks in the trump suit, count two tricks for king and queen, one trick for the king or the queen and knave, and one half of one trick for the queen or the knave, ten.

Both the opening bidder and the responder in valuing the side suits, credit themselves with half a trick for the fourth card of a four card suit with one trick for the two long cards of a five card suit and with two tricks for the three long cards of a six card suit. The responding hand can also take into account the ruffing value of his hand. Holding three cards in his partner's suit and only two cards in one of the side suits he can estimate the ruffing value in that suit as half a trick. With only one card in the side suit the estimated ruffing value is one trick, and with no card in one of the side suits it is two tricks. The reason the ruffing value is so low is that the opponents will be fully alive to the ruffing danger and will try to draw dummy's trumps before he can use them on their own good cards. If dummy has four trumps this danger is not so great and the ruffing value of the hand is increased. With four trumps and a doubleton suit it is safe to count on one ruffing trick, while with a singleton in a side suit there should be two ruffing tricks, and with a void, three ruffing tricks. In estimating the probable ruffing tricks only one short suit should be considered.

Some players are quite content to base their bidding entirely on honour tricks, but to secure greater accuracy it is far better to include also the playing trick value of the hand. To the beginner it always appears to make the game very difficult, when so much initial calculation is necessary, but in an incredibly short time the difficulties disappear. The good player can see at a glance what his hand is worth and it is only when the bidding has reached the higher ranges that involved calculations become necessary. In making an opening bid a player undertakes to make at least four tricks. With a hand which is above the average in honour strength, this is not an optimistic estimate and his bid is based upon the assumption that the remaining honour strength is divided. If this assumption is accurate each of the other three players may make three tricks. With four tricks in his own hand and three in his partner's hand a contract to make seven tricks should not be difficult. The partner knowing that the opening bid promises at least four tricks, estimates the probable number of playing cards in his own hand. He knows that the opener is relying on three tricks from him. With the suit already named as trumps he can see six probable playing tricks in his own hand and he knows at once that the partnership hands should be played in a game contract. The response which he gives must be so framed as to keep the bidding open. There are various methods by which this can be done and these will be discussed later. At the moment it is sufficient to point out that great responsibility rests upon the responder, he is not the mere dummy that he will become later. He has to make a bid which will give his partner some indication of his strength and ensure that the bidding will not be dropped before game is reached. The opening bid may have been made with the absolute minimum of honour and playing trick strength, in which case the opener will be anxious to drop the bidding at the earliest possible opportunity. On the other hand the opener may have a strong hand with far more playing tricks than indicated by a bid of one of a suit. In that case the partnership hands are probably capable of reaching the slam zone. One of the greatest problems of the game is so to direct the bidding that the partnership shall reach the best contract and for this a very large share of the responsibility rests upon the responder. It is not going too far to say that in a very large number of cases the failure to bid games and slams which are made but not bid, must be laid on the shoulders of the responder who has given too little thought to what he should say in the initial stages of the bidding.

When a side has scored a game it becomes vulnerable. This is important for it increases the penalty which goes to the opponents when the declarer fails to make his contract. When a side is not vulnerable the penalty is 50 points scored above the line by the opponents for each trick by which the declarer is short of his contract, while when vulnerable, the penalty is increased to 100 points. During the bidding it is open to any player when it is his turn to call, to double the last bid if made by an opponent. If the other players all pass, the hand is played in the doubled contract. If the declarer makes his contract—say Two Spades—he scores below the line double the value of his contract. In this case it would be 120 points which would give him game. In the 1948 Laws of Bridge, there is also a premium of 50 points scored above the line for making a doubled or redoubled contract. If the declarer fails in a doubled contract when not vulnerable, the penalty is 100 points for the first trick and 200 points for each subsequent trick by which he is short of his contract. If he is vulnerable, however, the penalty is 200 points for the first trick and 300 points for each subsequent trick. When a contract is doubled it is open to the bidder or his partner to re-double. If the contract is made, the value of each trick is redoubled so One No Trump or a bid of one in a major suit if redoubled would enable the declarer to make game. This rarely happens however, for the doubling side usually find an escape suit which they can bid and it may be cheaper for them to go down in a doubled contract than to leave in a redouble which would give their opponents game with possibly a bonus for overtricks. The premium value of overtricks in a doubled contract is 100 points each when not vulnerable and 200 points each when vulnerable. Redoubling doubles the premium points for overtricks.

Premiums are awarded for bidding and making slams. A little slam is a bid of Six No Trumps or six of a suit and a grand slam is a bid of seven. The little slam earns a premium of 500 points above the line if not vulnerable and 750 points if vulnerable. The grand slam premium is 1,000 points if not vulnerable and 1,500 points if vulnerable. There is of course no premium for a slam made but not bid.

There is also a premium for holding four aces in one hand at no trumps, or four or five honours in one hand in trumps at a suit contract. To many people it appears to be illogical that a player who is so fortunate as to be dealt good cards should receive a premium for what after all is merely the luck of the deal, but all attempts to abolish this premium have been unsuccessful. The premium is 150 points for holding four aces in one hand at no trumps and five honours in the trump suit in a suit contract. The honour cards are ace, king, queen, knave and ten of a suit. For holding four honours in trumps in one hand the premium is 100 points. This premium for honours can be scored by either side for, though it is rare, it happens occasionally that one of the opponents of the declarer holds four honours in the trump suit.

Although the premium for honours is attractive it should not be allowed to become an obsession. There are some average players who are inclined to regard the possession of four honours in their own hand as settling at once the suit in which it must be played. There have been many tragedies at the bridge table as a result of this obsession. North opens the bidding with One Heart. South with good support for hearts bids One Spade because he holds ace, king, queen, knave of the suit and continues to outbid his partner until the latter retires at a game bid of Four Spades. A contract of Four Hearts giving game and rubber could be made with ease, but the declarer is two down in Four Spades, losing 200 points on the hand less his premium of 100 points for honours. " I had to go on with spades for I had four honours," he will declare. The partner who will rarely refrain from pointing out that a score of 120 points for Four Hearts made plus rubber points of 500 is more profitable to the partnership than a net loss of 100 points, will not become any more sympathetic if on the next deal the opponents take game and rubber points.

It is sound advice therefore to suggest that too much importance should not be attached to the premium for honours. It pays frequently to forget all about it when a player has good support for his partner's suit and the bidding has made it clear that the partner does not like the suit in which the honours are held.

To the beginner the division of the score into two compartments, below the line and above the line, appears complicated at first but it is not really so. The only score to go below the line is that for tricks bid and made. All premiums and scores for tricks over or penalties for under tricks go above the line.

3

VALUING THE HAND

THE first essential when learning to play bridge is to acquire a thorough understanding of the bidding principles. This is not only necessary in order to secure that the partnership shall reach the best contract but also to enable the partners to find the best line of defence if an opponent becomes the declarer. From the very beginning there should be a realization of the importance of the partnership factor. Bridge is a partnership game. Each player is dealt thirteen cards, but the partnership holds twenty-six cards, and the whole object of the game is to secure that the best possible use is made of those cards. Here the declarer has a definite advantage, for he knows which of the twenty-six cards are held by the partnership, while each of the defenders is to a large extent in the dark about the particular cards held by his partner. A defender can see his own cards and those placed face upwards on the table by the dummy, and he can also deduce from the bidding that certain cards must be held by the declarer, but if there is no opposition bidding he has no guide to which of the missing cards likely to take tricks is held by his partner. While the declarer, knowing that important cards which may take tricks are held by an opponent, can plan his play to give himself the best chance to catch the missing cards or to reduce their trick taking possibilities, a defender can only assume that his partner may hold certain cards and has to study how to play to give the partnership the best chance to make them. At times, when the top cards are fairly evenly divided, there is opposition bidding which makes the planning of the defence easier, but as a general rule it will be found that the knowledge of the exact cards held in the partnership hands is worth at least one trick to the declarer.

Before the bidding starts it is necessary to know how to value the hand. Sound bidding is the basis of success at Bridge. A partner whose bidding can be relied upon thoroughly is likely to be welcomed in any Bridge circle. Certain requirements have been laid down as a guide to bidding and though there are occasions when these may be shaded, that is reduced slightly, by good players who can by expert card play make every possible trick in the partnership hands, the best advice that can be given to the novice and also to the average player is to be thoroughly conservative in bidding. If the partner is an expert, any shading can be left to him, but without expert knowledge shaded bidding only too frequently leads to disaster and the destruction of partnership confidence.

The first thing to learn if the hand is to be valued correctly for bidding purposes is its probable trick-taking value. Tricks are taken by honour cards, the long cards of a suit and by trumps. The honour cards are the ace, king, queen, knave, ten of a suit. The ace can usually be regarded as certain to take a trick and is valued as one honour trick, and the ace and king of the same suit as two honour-tricks. A king if accompanied by at least one other card but not the ace will take a trick if the ace of the suit is on its right, but it stands a very good chance of being killed if the ace is sitting over it. As it has an even chance of making a trick it is valued at half an honour trick.   Similarly with ace and queen of a suit in the same hand two tricks should be made if the king is on the right but only one if it is on the left, this combination is valued as one and one half honour tricks.   So also is king, queen, knave of a suit.   This may seem a conservative estimate for though the ace may kill one of the cards there appear to be two certain tricks left.   But unless these cards are in the trump suit the third round may be ruffed (trumped) so safety demands that this combination should count as only one plus.   Queen, knave and another card of the suit or two queens each with another card of the suit or one guarded king all count as half an honour trick.

In valuing his hand for bidding purposes a player's first consideration is honour tricks but he must also take into account its probable playing trick value, for only about eight of the thirteen tricks in each deal are taken by honour cards.   In estimating the playing trick value the opener counts every trump beyond three as one probable trick while in a side suit the fourth and fifth cards are regarded as half a trick each.   This estimate is based on the assumption that the partner will have trump support and may have to be revised, for if he does not support the suit the long cards in the trump suit should be given only the playing trick value of long cards in a side suit.

TABLE OF HONOUR-TRICKS

A.K. in the same suit	2
A.Q. in the same suit	1½
A.J.10.	1 plus
K.Q.J.	1 plus
A.	1
K.Q. in the same suit	1

K.J.10. in the same suit	1
K.x.	$\frac{1}{2}$
Q.J.x.	$\frac{1}{2}$

x means any small card of the same suit.

TABLE OF PLAYING TRICKS
Honours Winners

In declarer's hand when the trump suit has been supported by his partner.

	Winners
A.K.Q.	3
A.K.J.	$2\frac{1}{2}$
A Q.J.	2 plus
K.Q.J.	2
A.Q.10.	$1\frac{1}{2}$ plus
A.J.10.	$1\frac{1}{2}$
K.Q.10.	$1\frac{1}{2}$
A.J.	1 plus
K.Q.x.	1 plus
K.J.10.	1
Q.J.10.	1
K.J.	$\frac{1}{2}$ plus
Q.J.x.	$\frac{1}{2}$ plus

LONG SUIT WINNERS

If the trump suit is supported by the partner.

Length	Trumps	Side Suits
4 cards	1 trick	$\frac{1}{2}$ trick
5 cards	2 tricks	1 trick
6 cards	3 tricks	2 tricks
7 cards	4 tricks	4 tricks

Responder's Valuation

When supporting his partner's trump suit the responder can attach the following values to his trumps.

K.	1 trick
Q.	$\frac{1}{2}$ trick
J.10.	$\frac{1}{2}$ trick
Four cards	$\frac{1}{2}$ trick
Five cards	1 trick
Six cards	2 tricks

Ruffing Values

With 3 trumps and only two cards in a side suit $\frac{1}{2}$ trick, with 4 trumps, 1 trick.

With three trumps and a singleton in a side suit 1 trick, with 4 trumps 2 tricks.

With 3 trumps and a void in a side suit 2 tricks, with 4 trumps 3 tricks.

Trick Taking Expectancy

In order to keep their bidding on sound lines, players should have some knowledge of the trick taking expectancy of the partnership hands.

The opening bid gives a clear indication of the minimum of honour strength held by the player who makes it. A response by the partner also shows that he has at least the minimum strength indicated by his bid. Both partners now therefore have a clear idea of the minimum honour strength in the combined hands, which will enable them to close the bidding at or near the safety level. But either or both may have hands which are much stronger than have been shown by their first bids.

To guide them in their further bidding they have the knowledge that if the strength in the combined hands is from four to five honour tricks they can usually be sure of the odd trick in a trump contract, with from five to five and a half honour tricks they should make one no trump or two of a suit and with a long solid trump suit and a good fit, may be able to make game in a major suit contract. With six honour tricks in the combined hands there should usually be a game in either a suit or no trumps and with six and a half to eight honour tricks the partnership is in the slam zone. For those who prefer to use the point count, four for an ace, three for a king, two for a queen and one for a knave, a count of 23-24 in the combined hands should enable Two No Trumps to be made, 26 should enable Three No Trumps to be made, and 33 or more should produce a small slam in No Trumps. When the opening bid is One No Trump the responder assumes that it has been made on the minimum count, and with seven or eight points responds Two No Trumps. If the opener had the bare minimum required for his bid he will pass, but if he has more points than he has shown he may bid Three No Trumps. Although 26 points is given here as the requirement for bidding Three No Trumps, nine tricks can frequently be made with a lower count in the combined hands if one of the partners has a long and quickly establishable suit or if both hands are well filled with intermediate cards. In the early stages of bridge, however, it is advisable to adhere strictly to the honour or point count laid down.

The distributional count which gives the playing tricks valuation of the combined hands is very useful as a guide, for it gives a good indication how far the bidding can be

B

carried with safety.   It introduces complications however for the responder in supporting an opening bid in a
trump suit can value the king of that suit as one trick,
the queen or knave, ten or four cards in the suit as half a
trick. If the responder, instead of supporting his partner's
suit bids a suit of his own, the opener has to re-value his
hand as though he was the responder.   He can no longer
attach the same value to the suit he has bid, but must
treat it as a side suit, reducing the value of the fourth
card to half a trick.   On the other hand the king, queen,
or knave, ten of his partner's suit take on additional trick
values.

4

OPENING SUIT BIDS OF ONE

To open the bidding a player should have a biddable suit if he proposes to play in a trump contract, or honour strength in all suits if he elects to play in no trumps. For a suit contract there should be three honour tricks if the trump suit contains only four cards and two and a half honour tricks if the trump suit has five cards. A biddable suit is one which if containing only four cards should have two honours higher than the ten, if containing five cards one honour higher than the ten. If the proposed trump suit has six cards or more it can be bid even if it has no honour card, for the extra length gives a promise of long card tricks which makes it possible to dispense with the requirement that there should be at least one high card in the suit.

While the beginner should be very careful to ensure that his opening bids are sound, he should guard against excessive caution. If he has the requirements for an opening bid he should bid. If he does not tell his partner at once that he has better than an average hand he will find it very difficult to convince him in the subsequent bidding that he has the strength which his bidding shows. The psychological effect of saying No Bid when he first takes part in the auction may also have an adverse effect on the partnership. A player with a borderline hand, hesitating whether or not to open the bidding, will reflect that as his partner had not bid there is little or no prospect of making a game, while if all the strength is held by

opponents a penalty is likely to be incurred.   He may
pass therefore, and when the cards are thrown in may discover that a game has been missed.   If he decides to take
the risk and opens with One Spade, the responder may
make the strong call of Three Spades.   Though this bid
is strongly invitational the knowledge that the responder
could not open the bidding may induce the opener to pass
and a game which could have been made is not bid.
Again when both opponents have bid it is much more
difficult for the fourth player, who may possibly have as
good cards as either of them, to interfere in the bidding.
There are many occasions too when the opponents will
secure the declaration where an opening bid made by a
defender gives the other defender guidance both for the
opening lead and the formulation of the best line of
defence.

The opening bid and the partner's response are two of
the most important things in bridge.   When both are
sound there is little fear of partnership crashes which so
terrify the novice and are so destructive of confidence.
The vast majority of the opening bids made are bids of
one.   It is only when a player picks up a power house or a
rock crusher, as hands of exceptional strength are termed,
or where he has absolutely freak distribution, that there is
any advantage to be gained from opening with a higher
bid than one.   In the early days of contract bridge the
opening bid was much more simple than it is today.   Now
before he makes his opening bid a player has to give some
thought to his possible re-bid.   The one-over-one system
of bidding which has been adopted fairly generally provides that if the first or second bidder opens with one of a
suit and his partner responds with a bid in another suit,
that response is forcing for one round and the opener

must bid again.   This applies only to opening bids when
the responder has had no previous opportunity to bid.
If the opening bid is made by the third or fourth bidder
the change of suit is no longer forcing, for the initial pass
by the ultimate responder has shown that his hand cannot
be very strong.

With two long suits of equal length, bid first the higher
ranking even though it may be the weaker suit.   On the
next round bid the second suit.   Distributional value
plays a very important part in the game and can go a long
way to compensate for the absence of honour strength.
To take an extreme case it may be possible owing to
favourable distribution, to make thirteen tricks, with two
aces and three kings in the hands of the opponents.   The
opening bidder holds ♠—8.7.6.5.4.3.2. ♡—— . ♢—— .
♣—A.K.Q.J.7.2.   Though he has only two honour
tricks he opens with the longer of his two suits bidding
One Spade.   The responder with ♠—A.Q.9. ♡—
J.10.8.7. ♢—Q.8.4.2. ♣—10.4. will bid Two Spades
and whatever action the opponents may take the hands
will be played in at least a game contract in spades.   If
the outstanding spades are divided 2–1 as they will be
78 times in 100 it is only necessary to find the king on the
declarer's left to make 13 tricks.

With 7–6 distribution the seven card suit is bid first and
the six card suit on the next round of the bidding.   On
the third round the opener should re-bid the six card suit.
This re-bid tells the responder that the second suit bid is
at least a five card suit and that the first suit bid must be at
least of the same length.   If the opening bid has been
One Diamond and the first re-bid One Spade, the responder, knowing that with two suits of equal length the
higher valued suit would have been bid first, is able

when the spades are re-bid to place his partner with at least six diamonds and five spades. It is obvious to him that the opener can have no support for any suit he may bid and unless he has a long solid suit of his own, his duty is to support the long suit in the opener's hand which best fits the partnership hands. With 7–4 or 6–4 distribution, the six or seven card suit should be bid and re-bid before the four card suit is bid. There may be times however, when it is more convenient and saves raising the level of the bidding to show the four card suit before re-bidding the six card suit. With ♠—A.K.J.4. ♡—J.8. ◇—A.Q.10.9.6.3. ♣—7, the opening bid is One Diamond. If the response is One Heart a bid of One Spade shows the second suit at the level of one. The opener can show his greater length in diamonds later by re-bidding the suit. There are times too when with 6–5 distribution it is more convenient to bid a five card major suit before a six card minor suit. In some systems of bidding it is the rule with 6–5 distribution to open the bidding with the higher ranking suit, the theory being, that if the partner holds three cards in the suit a five card trump suit can be set up almost as easily as a six card suit. Here however, we are not considering special bids of special systems, and in normal approach forcing bidding, the aim should be to avoid deceiving the partner. With a solid five card major suit and a somewhat ragged six card minor suit it is sometimes advisable to open with the major suit rather than the longer minor suit, but it is usually better to avoid making any bid which will give the partner wrong information.

With two biddable five card suits the opening bid should be made in the higher ranking suit. The higher ranking suit is bid first because when the second suit is shown the responder, if he prefers the first suit bid, can show his preference without raising the level of the bidding. For example South holding ♠—Q.J.10.7.6. ♡—A.K.10.7.3. ◊—5. ♣—A.5. would bid One Spade. North with ♠—9.8.5. ♡—8.4. ◊—A.K.Q.7.2. ♣—J.9.6.4. would respond Two Diamonds. South would now show his second suit with Two Hearts and North with three cards in spades and only two cards in hearts will show his preference for the suit first bid by saying Two Spades. South has now little difficulty in bidding and making Four Spades. If for his opening bid South had chosen One Heart because that suit was stronger than his spades, he would have had to bid Two Spades over the response of Two Diamonds. Now when North has to bid, should his preference be for hearts, he would have to raise the bidding to the three level and on some occasions at least, eight tricks may be the maximum the partnership hands can make. With a biddable five card suit and a biddable four card suit the five card suit should be bid first.

In making an opening bid a player announces that he has better than an average hand, and his partner knows that he can assume that it will take at least four tricks. It requires seven tricks to make a contract of one and when he makes his opening bid a player assumes that the cards to take the nine tricks which with his own four add up to 13 are evenly divided. In bidding one of a suit, or one no trump with a minimum hand, therefore a player is running a risk that his partner has a completely worthless hand and that he may incur a penalty which if he is vulnerable may be as large as 800 points. For this reason it is better when vulnerable to exercise some caution about opening the bidding with a bare minimum and unless the hand contains good intermediate cards which may be developed into winners, it may be wiser to pass on the first round and to come into the bidding strongly if the partner should open. Even when not vulnerable the mere possession of three honour tricks does not entitle a player to make an opening bid. For instance holding ♠—A.3.2. ♡—A.5.2. ◇—A.7.3. ♣—8.7.6.4. the hand contains three honour tricks but it does not constitute an opening bid. It is however a very strong supporting hand, and if the partner is able to open the bidding it very greatly increases the playing trick strength of the partnership hands. King, queen combinations in the opener's hand, which he has valued at one playing trick, will produce two tricks in the suits of which his partner has the aces and the additional controls which the aces give will be of great value in the development of long cards. To open the bidding the partner must have had two and a half to three honour tricks, and assuming that he has a minimum of two and a half honour tricks there are at least five and a half in the partnership hands. Four honour tricks in the partnership hands should produce a part score, five and a half honour tricks and a good fit in trumps should produce game in a major suit, six honour tricks should give game in no trumps or in a suit, while six and a half to eight honour tricks place the partnership in the slam zone. With this knowledge the holder of the hand containing three aces can see that when his partner opens the bidding the partnership is in the game zone unless the opener has an absolute minimum. If the opening bid has been One Spade, One Heart, or One Diamond, he can safely jump to three of the suit if he has good trump support. As he has previously said No Bid this is not forcing and may be passed, but if the opener has more than a minimum he will accept the invitation and bid game in a major suit or no trumps. If the opening bid had been One Club the response would have been Two No Trumps.

The great majority of the hands upon which an opening bid is made suggest as trumps a suit of which the opener has only four cards and it is these hands to which the one-over-one obligation presents the greatest difficulty. Before making an opening bid a player has to consider the probable response from his partner and, if possible, how he can so direct the bidding that the re-bid he will be called upon to make if his partner changes the suit will cause him the least embarrassment. He no longer opens automatically his higher ranking suit but considers how, while keeping the bidding as low as possible, he can convey to his partner some indication of the character of his hand. Take an extreme case where the opener has three biddable four card suits : ♠—A.Q.10.6. ♡—A.Q.10.3. ◇—5. ♣—Q.J.3.2. With 4-4-4-1 distribution he has to select one of his four card suits. Which shall he choose ? Experience has proved that the best bid is the suit below his own short suit. This after all is merely common sense. The most probable response is a bid of one in the suit of which he is short. The opening bid therefore is One Club and when his partner bids One Diamond the re-bid is One Spade. If the partner now bids Two Diamonds the opener can bid Two Hearts. If the opener's hand is slightly different : ♠—A.Q.10.6. ♡—A.Q.10.3. ◇—Q.J.3.2. ♣—5., there is no suit of lower value than clubs but this difficulty is met by opening with One Spade. If the response is Two Clubs the opener can bid Two Hearts. The responder is at liberty to pass this bid for it is not forcing though it is

B*

a change of suit. With a minimum response he will pass if his hearts are better than his spades but with better spades than hearts he can put the opener back into spades without increasing the number of tricks which will have to be made. With more than a minimum he will keep the bidding open.

Two Four Card Suits

With two four card biddable suits the position is more difficult. If the suits are touching, i.e. next in value to each other as with spades and hearts, hearts and diamonds, diamonds and clubs, it is better to bid the higher ranking first. The lower ranking suit can then be shown on the second round and the responder can take the opener back into the suit first bid without increasing the contract. If the opener has ♠—A.Q.10.6. ♡—A.K.10.3. ◇—Q.9. ♣—J.8.7., the bidding would be One Spade and if the response was Two Clubs the opener's second bid would be Two Hearts. The responder with a preference for spades would now bid two of that suit. If however the opening bid had been One Heart, and over Two Clubs the re-bid had been Two Spades, the responder who prefers hearts to spades would have to bid at the level of three to put the opener back into that suit.

If the suits are not touching, the general rule is to open with the biddable suit below the singleton or doubleton. There are occasions however when it is wise to depart from this rule. These sometimes occur when the non-touching suits are spades and diamonds or hearts and clubs and the opener is weak in the other two suits. Mr. Culbertson the great apostle of preparedness recommends that on hands of this type with minimum strength the stronger suit should be opened first. With ♠—A.K.J.6. ♡—8.3. ◇—K.J.10.5. ♣—6.3.2., the recommended opening bid is One Spade not One Diamond. If the response is Two Clubs the re-bid is Two Diamonds. If however the responder says Two Hearts over the opening bid of One Spade, the re-bid should be Two Spades. Here if the bid had been One Diamond and the response Two Clubs the opener would have found it difficult to re-bid, for it would be dangerous to bid his spades for the first time at the range of two.

The Fishing Club

If the opener has strength in three suits the position is very different. In the above hand give the opener the ace of clubs instead of the six, and a Two Hearts response to One Spade will no longer embarrass him for he can now bid Two No Trumps while if the response is Two Clubs he can raise to Three Clubs or bid Two Diamonds.

It is one of the contradictions of bridge, that having had it impressed upon us over and over again that to open the bidding we must have a biddable suit of at least four cards and that a biddable four card suit should have at least two cards higher than the ten, we find that there are occasions when we are expected to open with a bid of one of a suit which may be no stronger than Q.3.2. This opening bid of a three card suit is only made in a minor suit. Introduced originally to meet the difficulty experienced with hands sufficiently strong to open the bidding but with the strength so distributed that it was difficult to find an opening bid or possibly to find a re-bid it has become very popular. The " Fishing Club " as it has been termed is used largely in some circles to indicate a light no trump holding and to explore the possibilities at a low level. The type of hand for which it is designed is : ♠—A.K.10.8. ♡—Q.10.6. ◇—10.8.5. ♣—K.8.6. Here if the opening bid is One Spade and the response Two Diamonds, it would not be easy to find a safe re-bid but with an opening bid of One Club and a response of One Diamond there is a re-bid of One Spade.

This opening bid in a three card minor suit is very useful when the partner has had no opportunity to bid and the opener will be called upon to bid again after any response. If the partner has already passed, the opener is under no obligation to find a re-bid and can therefore bid his hand naturally. Third or fourth in hand therefore holding ♠—A.K.10.8. ♡—Q.10.6. ◇—10.8.5. ♣—K.8.6., an opening bid of One Spade is to be preferred to a bid of One Club on a three card suit. His partner being unable to open the bidding, it is most unlikely that the partnership hands will produce game and all that can be expected is a part score. If over a third or fourth hand bid of One Spade there is a response of Two Hearts, Two Diamonds or Two Clubs the auction can be allowed to die.

5

RESPONSES TO ONE OF A SUIT

In the early stages of bridge, opening bids and responses must be perfectly sound. Shaded bids, that is bids made on hands which just fail to satisfy the normal requirements, may be made by experts whose skill in the play of the cards entitles them to take risks but these bids are not safe for novices. The only sound rule for the beginner is to be sure that he has the full strength which is required for the bid which he makes. If his partner is an expert he can do any shading which may be called for, and the knowledge that he can rely on the soundness of the novices' bid will be invaluable to him.

The beginner at bridge should learn thoroughly the requirements for the various responses he should make to his partner's opening bid. All that he knows when he has to consider his first response is that his partner has a hand which is better than the average and that he has a biddable suit. The opening bid may have been made on a hand containing only the minimum strength required, but it is possible that it may have been made on a hand so strong that it requires little help from him to make game. It is his duty if possible to make some bid which will give his partner a chance to bid again and in making his response he has to consider how he can best indicate to the opener the character of his own hand. If his hand is very weak, he is in no difficulty : he will pass. This confession of extreme weakness may encourage the opponent on his left to put in a bid, but unless he does so the opener may be deprived of an opportunity to show a second suit which would provide a much better fit for the partnership hands. If he has only so little as one honour trick in his hand therefore, the responder should consider whether he cannot make some bid.

In considering what bid he should make, the responder should first take into account what support he has for the suit bid by his partner. Adequate trump support for his partner's suit is three cards headed by ace, king, queen or knave and ten, or four small cards. If he has that support he has the necessary honour strength to enable him to bid. To make a single raise in the suit his hand should contain one and a half honour tricks with trump support. Even without adequate trump support the responder should endeavour to find a bid. Though a one-over-one response—One Diamond, One Heart or One Spade over One Club, One Heart or One Spade over One Diamond or One Spade over One Heart—is forcing for one round it can be made with very little honour strength. A six card suit can be bid with only half an honour trick in the hand, a five card suit with one honour trick in the hand or a four card suit with one plus honour trick in the hand. A two-over-one response requires more strength, for it increases the number of tricks which have to be made. To make a two-over-one response the hand should contain one and a half honour tricks with a six card suit, two honour tricks with a five card suit and two and a half honour tricks with a four card suit.

There are many occasions when the responder has neither adequate support for the suit bid by his partner nor a biddable suit of his own but must keep the bidding open if he can. If he has only one honour trick and that is in one suit only, he should pass, but if that honour

trick is made up of cards in two suits he should bid One
No Trump. This is recognised as a weak bid, for One
No Trump should not be bid with more than two plus
honour tricks in the hand. If there are one and a half
honour tricks or more, it is no longer necessary for the
honour cards to be in more than one suit. A single
raise in the partner's suit or a bid of One No Trump
after the partner has bid a suit are not regarded as encouraging and the opener is not likely to bid again unless
he has a second suit which may provide a better fit, or
has a much stronger hand than he has shown by his
opening bid. If the opener does bid again there is no
obligation on the responder to keep the bidding open,
but he should endeavour to do so. He knows now that
his partner must have a strong hand and may require
very little help from him to make game. This knowledge
gives him a more optimistic outlook and encourages him
to strain a point to keep the bidding open. Very often
the opener's second suit is one which he can support. If
for example South opens with a bid of One Spade, North
holding ♠—7.4. ♡—10.9.8.6. ◇—A.Q.6. ♣—Q.J.9.6.
will respond One No Trump. South now bids Two
Hearts and North with adequate trump support for the
new suit bid by his partner can raise to Three Hearts.
If, however, North's cards are ♠—8.7.6. ♡—10.9.6.
◇—A.Q.6. ♣—Q.J.9.6. his second response will be
Two Spades on the assumption that spades being the
first suit bid by his partner it may be his longer or stronger suit. South will not interpret this bid as showing
normal support for spades, for it merely indicates that
his spades are equal in value to his hearts. This switch
back to spades has the additional advantage that it keeps
the bidding open without increasing the number of

tricks the declarer is contracting to make. With a weaker hand for example, ♠—7. ♡—10.9.8.6. ◇—A.10.6.2. ♣—Q.9.6.2. The response to an opening bid of One Spade would still be One No Trump, but when the opener bids Two Hearts the responder would be satisfied that the partnership had found a trump suit in which a part score could be made and would say " No bid."

So far we have been dealing with responses with weak hands but very often the responder has considerable· strength. Of the four players at the table the responder knows the most about the prospects and is best fitted to direct the bidding in the right direction. By making an opening bid the opener has indicated that he has better than an average hand but he has not taken command of the partnership. He merely indicates that he has a biddable suit and a certain number of honour cards. He is prepared to play the partnership hands with the suit named as trumps, but he is ready to consider anything his partner can tell him about his own hand. The best response to make to the opening bid is not always easy to find. The responder if he has a strong hand can see that there is almost certainly a game possible on the partnership hands. He may have a hand on which he would have opened the bidding if the players taking part in the auction before him had passed and he knows that with an opening bid opposite there is usually a game in the partnership hands. He must therefore so steer the bidding that it is kept open until game is reached. If he has good support for his partner's suit and a good suit of his own, he has to consider whether to support his partner immediately, or to bid his own suit. There is one case at least in which a player holding nine cards in one suit headed by the four top honours, refrained deliberately from showing it in the bidding. His cards were: ♠—K.J.7.2. ♣—A.K.Q.J.9.8.7.4.2. and his partner opened the bidding with One Spade. His response was Five No Trumps, the grand slam force, a conventional bid which called upon the opener to bid Seven Spades if he had two of the three top honours in the suit. He had and the grand slam was bid and made. As a general rule however, the responder has no such spectacular course open to him. If the opening bid has been one of a major suit and his own strong suit is a minor a jump bid to three in his partners' suit may be better than showing his own suit. If the opening bid has been one of a minor suit it is usually better to show a biddable major suit even with good support for the minor. It is easier to make game in a major suit. With a very strong hand he can make a forcing to game bid by a jump bid in another suit, and this has definite advantages, for it tells the opening bidder that if he has any additional strength the partnership may be in the slam zone.

If the responding hand has no support for the suit named by his partner, but has a biddable suit of his own he should bid it. The opener may not be at all keen on the suit he has bid and it is quite possible that he would prefer to play in a no trump contract but is afraid to do so because of his own weakness in one of the suits. Should his partner by bidding that suit show that he has some strength in it, the objection to no trumps disappears and a game bid in no trumps may be the best contract. It may be that the opener can support the suit bid by the responder and if it is a major suit he should support it as strongly as he is able to do. As has been pointed out, it is a frequent fault of the average player to be obsessed by the sight of four honours in his own hand in the suit he has bid and he will insist upon playing in that suit even though he can support his partner's suit. The premium of 100 points awarded for holding four honours in the trump suit in one hand is a nice addition to the score, but it is a thoroughly unsound proceeding to insist upon playing in your own suit in order to score the premium for honours when by supporting the suit bid by your partner a game contract could have been reached. Yet over and over again we see this happen. One partner, for example will open with One Spade and will receive a response of Two Hearts from his partner. The opener will see that he has good support for his partner's heart suit but instead of bidding Three Hearts or Four Hearts will bid Two Spades because with four honours in the suit in his own hand he is obsessed by the thought of the 100 point premium. Having no support for spades the partner will now pass. If the contract is made, 60 points will be scored below the line and 100 points above the line. But game in hearts has been missed and this is a very poor result, for the invisible value of the first game is 300 points, and of the second game, if the opponents are not vulnerable, 400 points more. A score of 160 points for making Two Spades with four honours in one hand may look attractive on the score sheet but when 100 points are above the line and only 60 points count towards game, it is a poor substitute for 120 points below the line which have a value of 300 points in addition though those points are not shown on the score sheet. The premium for honours is sometimes useful when a player has to decide whether or not he should make a sacrifice bid, for it will reduce by

100 or 150 points the penalty incurred but there are many cases in which it is wise to ignore this premium. The great aim of a partnership should be to reach and make the best contract.

6

OPENING NO TRUMP BIDS AND RESPONSES

THE most popular method of hand valuation for No Trump bidding is the Milton Work count of four for an Ace, three for a King, two for a Queen and one for a Jack. Tens and even nines play their part and many players allow half a point for every ten. These intermediate cards assume a far greater importance than in a suit contract where the value of setting up a long card in a suit is less in evidence. This method of hand valuation has largely superseded the old Culbertson quick trick valuation.

One No Trump should be bid on a balanced distribution which means a four four three two or four three three three or even five three three two division of the cards held in each suit. Occasionally a six three two two pattern may be allowed when the six card suit is either clubs or diamonds. In the latter case the doubleton suits must be headed by the Ace or King. The even distribution of the cards is important, for if the responder should decide that there is a game in the partnership hands, but that it will play better in a trump suit owing to his own unbalanced distribution, he should rely on finding at least three cards of that suit or two with a high honour in the opener's hand.

When One No Trump is bid with a five or six card suit it is usually because the opener has a long and nearly solid minor suit with guarded honours in the other suits and can see the possibilities of making the nine tricks required for game at No Trumps, but possibly not the eleven tricks necessary in a trump contract.

The opening bid of One No Trump has the very definite advantage that the responder can see at once the possibilities of the partnership cards. He knows that the opener has a certain specified strength according to whether the partnership is playing the weak (13-15) or the strong (16-18) point No Trumps and that he has a balanced distribution with honour cards in every suit. If he has a strong suit in which he thinks that it would be better to play for game than in No Trumps, he can count on adequate support for that suit. He can attach more value to his own honour cards knowing that his patner can fill to some extent gaps in each suit. He should know that with 25-26 points in the combined hands it is usually possible to make game in No Trumps and by adding his own honour strength to that shown by his partner he can estimate at once whether game is likely. The responses to No Trump bids will be set out later.

EXAMPLES FOR NO TRUMP OPENING BIDS

The opening bid of One No Trump is the most popular and probably the most abused bid in bridge. It is also the bid which is subject to the most differences of opinion. Whatever the system employed nearly all players use as their basis the Milton Work count and therefore the combined strength of the hands can be estimated. Some hold the theory that because over One No Trump opponents must bid at the two level, an opening bid of One No Trump should be made on any type of ragged holding of between twelve and fourteen points. They are wrong because they forget that if doubled they too may have to submit to being rescued by their partners on a worthless hand or be resigned to taking very few tricks in One No Trump.   Remember the one really effective double at the one level is that of One No Trump.   Others prefer an intermediate course such as the Acol system advocates.   They bid a No Trump not vulnerable on 13-15 points and strengthen it when vulnerable to 16-18.   Their calculation is merely the mathematical one of how much it can cost.

The great majority, with whom I am in agreement, prefer the strong No Trump (16-18) throughout.   This is in line with the old Culbertson No Trump which was bid on three and a half to four honour tricks plus.   Suffice it is to say that over the past number of years every world ranking player has experimented with every form of No Trump bidding and all have eventually discarded the weak No Trump opening.

While 25-26 points between the two hands should normally produce a game, this does not always work out exactly for it is of course affected by distribution.   It is possible for game to be made with fewer points if a long suit in either hand can be set up while with the cards badly placed or inadequate guards in all suits declarer may fail with more than twenty-six points.   The following are typical One No Trump opening bids.

S. A Q x	Q 10 9	Q J x
H. K Q x	A J 10 x	K x x
D. A J x	K 10 x x	A Q x x
C. J 10 x x	A Q	A Q 10
(17 points)	(16 points)	(18 points)

Responses to One No Trump should normally be made

by adding the point count held, to the maximum of eighteen. That is to say with seven to eight points bid Two No Trumps. Partner with a maximum will bid Three and will pass with a minimum. With any less, pass, as six plus the maximum eighteen will produce only twenty-four. Holding nine points bid Three No Trumps as nine plus the minimum of sixteen should give a good play for game.

Holding

	(1)	(2)	(3)
S.	K 10 x	K x x	K x x
H.	x x x	x x	Q x
D.	x x x x	K J x x x	10 x x x
C.	K J 10	x x x	K J x x

With hands one and two raise One No Trump to Two. With hand three raise to Three No Trumps.

These requirements can be shaded considerably if a long suit is held, as with

S. J x x
H. x x
D. x x
C. A Q 10 x x x

raise One No Trump directly to Three.

The above examples take no account of unbalanced hands. That is hands containing five or six cards in a suit with a singleton or void. In these cases the suit should be bid as a warning that the responding hand is unsuitable for No Trumps unless the opening hand has a double guard in each of the unbid suits. The idea of a weakness take out should be discarded. Any response made should be prepared for a further bid from partner and must be regarded as constructional.   Holding three cards of the suit bid, if it should be a major suit, opener should support at once or otherwise re-bid Two No Trumps.   If the bid has been made on a broken six card suit responder should now sign off with three of the suit or even four.

For example holding

> S.   K J 10 x x x
> H.   x
> D.   K x x x
> C.   x x

On the bidding One No Trump, Two Spades, Two No Trumps responder should re-bid Four Spades but with

> S.   K x x x x x
> H.   x
> D.   Q J x x
> C.   x x

re-bid only Three Spades.

OPENING TWO NO TRUMPS BID

An opening bid of Two No Trumps shows a very strong hand which requires very little help from the responder to make game and if the responder has even moderate strength, the partnership may be in the slam zone.   The strength required for a Two No Trump bid is from 20 to 22 points, but if there are only 20 points the hand should contain several intermediate cards such as 10's and nines.

Every suit should be stopped and as a rule there should be 4-3-3-3 distribution.   The distributional require-

ment may be modified in special circumstances. With
4-4-3-2 distribution the doubleton suit must be at
least ace, knave. There are some hands containing a
long solid suit on which there may appear to be a good
prospect of making nine tricks in No Trumps, but the
holder may fear that game in a trump suit will be much
more difficult. The long suit must contain at least five
cards and should be a minor suit. There should be a
stopper in every suit and to guard against the danger that
the partner will force the bidding up to a slam, a bid of
Two No Trumps should be avoided unless he has already
shown that he has only moderate strength by passing.
Provided that the opener is satisfied that all these conditions are satisfied he may shade the strength and distributional requirements to 20 points with 5-3-3-2 distribution. Very occasionally also with 19/20 points and
6-3-2-2 distribution an opening bid of Two No Trumps
may be made, but every suit must be stopped and the
six card minor suit must be headed by ace, king, queen.

Responses To Two No Trumps

The opening bid of Two No Trumps has announced
that the hand is so powerful that little help is required to
raise it to game. With less than 4 points the responder
will pass but with 4 or more he will raise to Three No
Trumps. Even with only two queens in the hand the
responder is strong enough to bid Three No Trumps.
With a five card minor suit headed by at least the queen
and four cards in one of the major suits, a suit take
out is recommended, for if the opener can bid three
of the major suit held by the responder the partnership
hands may play better in that suit than in No Trumps.

With a five card major suit headed by at least the queen, even though he has only 4 points the responder should bid three of his major suit. If the opener now bids three of the other major suit the responder will sign off with a bid of Three No Trumps. The Two No Trump bid should be taken out into three of a major suit even without 4 points if the responder has six cards in the suit. If the opener now bids Three No Trumps the responder should re-bid his major suit. His hand would be useless in a No Trump contract but would take several tricks if his long major suit was the trump suit. With a six card minor suit of the same kind the responder should only bid the minor suit if the opponents doubled the opening bid. The opening bid of Two No Trumps is so powerful that very little is required in the responding hand to justify hopes of making a slam. Even with so little as 6 points, but with a six card major suit headed by ace or king, queen, the responder is justified in making a slam try by jumping at once to Four Spades. This jump to game should not be regarded as discouraging, for with a weaker hand the responder would have been content to bid three of his suit. With balanced distribution and 10 or 12 points, the responder should take out the Two No Trumps by a bid of three in his best suit and if the opener now bids either four of that suit or Three No Trumps the responder should indicate his strength by bidding Four No Trumps. This bid should not be mistaken for the conventional Four No Trump bid asking about aces, which is so useful in slam bidding, but it must be read as showing strength in the responding hand which makes a slam almost a certainty if the opening bid has not been shaded.

OPENING BIDS OF THREE NO TRUMPS

Opening bids of Three No Trumps are made with 23-25 points equivalent to six and a half to seven honour tricks. Opening bids of Four No Trump or Six No Trumps can be disregarded as modern bidding methods have removed their usefulness.

It must also be stated that the modern tendency is to open a Three No Trump bid as a semi-bluff holding a low point count but a long solid minor suit and a few scattered honour cards outside.

e.g.   K x
                    Q x
                    A K Q J x x x
                    K x

CONCERNING THE WEAK NO TRUMP

While a strong No Trump has been recommended there are nevertheless a number of players who still prefer to open No Trump on all hands which contain a minimum opening bid (12-14) points and a balanced distribution. Since it may be assumed that the reader is likely to encounter a great variety of styles and systems a short discussion of this type of bid appears relevant.

Referring to the weak No Trump opening here are a few examples of hands on which the bid might well be made.

(1)	(2)	(3)
S. Q 10 x	S. K x x	S. A x x
H. A J x	H. J 10 x	H. K J x x
D. K x x	D. A K x x	D. K J x
C. Q J x x	C. J 10 x	C. Q 10 x
(13 points)	(12 points)	(14 points)

Example (2) is a very minimum holding and it would be an unwise bid to make if vulnerable since the possibilities for a resounding double are all too apparent and no convenient rescue is available. Example (4) might offer a safer solution, leaving the aggressive nature of the bid, which its sponsors claim as its main advantage, unimpaired.

(4)

S. K x
H. J x
D. A K x x x x
C. J 10

Now it becomes quite obvious that opposite a weak No Trump opening partner's responses must vary from those given to a strong No Trump. For example, opposite a thirteen point No Trump a count of twelve is normally necessary for game to be a reasonable proposition. With this count or more a bid of Three No Trumps is justified.

These are example hands where a raise to Three No Trumps over a weak No Trump is justified.

(1)	(2)	(3)
S. A 10 x	S. J 10 x x	S. K Q x
H. J 10 x	H. A x	H. J x x x
D. A Q x x	D. K J x x x	D. K J x
C. J x x	C. K x	C. A x x

Raise to Two No Trumps on such hands as

(1)	(2)
S. K x x	S. A K x
H. Q J x	H. 10 x x x
D. K J x	D. Q x x
C. J x x x	C. Q x x

Partner will raise to game if he has 14 points.

This type of No Trump response is purely mathematical, as in response to the strong No Trump, and can be made automatically by merely agreeing with partner as to what type of No Trump bid is being used. Add the maximum to your own count and if the score is 25 or more then it is your duty to support partner in the hopes that he has a maximum hand. Conversely, should your count added to the minimum produce 25 or more then bid a direct Three No Trumps. It is nevertheless the responses on weak distributional hands that constitute the main difference in the handling of weak and strong No Trumps. Whereas the strong No Trump can stand on its own feet and rely on taking sufficient tricks in a One No Trump contract opposite a weak hand to relieve responder from the necessity of bidding on minimum values, there is no such comforting assurance opposite a weak No Trump where the penalty incurred in playing in One No Trump can be considerable. It is therefore assumed that a response at the Two level opposite a strong No Trump is an encouraging bid though not a completely forcing one. The response at the Two level opposite a weak No Trump should be taken as a complete sign off and the opening bidder should refrain from bidding again. The sole object of the bid is to warn partner and to seek a safer contract while at the same time making it more difficult for the opponents who may well have to pass on good hands or risk entering the bidding at the Three level.

Examples of hands where a response of two spades would be in order opposite a 12-14 point No Trump.

(1)	(2)	(3)
S. Q 10 9 x x	S. J 10 x x x	S. K J x x x
H. K x x	H. A x	H. x
D. x x x x	D. x x x	D. Q x x x
C. x	C. x x	C. x x x

Before closing the No Trump discussions it is well to draw the reader's attention to the most popularly used convention of the present day invented originally by the late S. J. Simon, but more readily referred to as the " Stayman Convention " out of courtesy to the American champion mainly responsible for its development. The idea of this being that the partner of the No Trump bidder with four cards in both major suits and the requisite strength to play the combined hands at the Two level should bid Two Clubs which is conventional and bears no relationship to the club suit, but asks partner to bid his lowest four-card major suit. If he does not hold one he will have to reply Two Diamonds or Two No Trumps and the hand must be played in a minimum of Two No Trumps.

Hands which qualify for such responses are of the following type:—

	(1)		(2)		(3)
S.	K J x x	S.	A 10 x x	S.	Q J x x
H.	Q 10 x x	H.	K J x x	H.	A x x
D.	x x x	D.	J x x x	D.	K x
C.	J x	C.	x	C.	x x x x

In all examples the major suit response will be passed except in example three where a Two Heart bid will be converted to Two No Trumps. On hand (2) a Two Diamond reply may be passed but in all other circumstances the hands will be played in Two No Trumps.

The bid can also be made opposite a strong No Trump, but its value has been proved to be less evident.

7

THE OPENING FORCING TWO-BID

THERE are some hands which are so strong that it is not safe to make a normal opening bid, for the partner with very little strength in his hand might pass. To deal with these hands which practically guarantee a game, no matter how weak the partner may be, a number of what are known as forcing bids are employed to compel the partner to keep the bidding open until game is reached. In the Forcing Approach System, an opening bid of two of a suit is the best known, and most abused, forcing bid. It requires great strength, for the opening bidder must be prepared to make game even if his partner has a bust, and a bust is a hand which has no trick taking value at all. The strength required to make an opening two-bid which is forcing to game is so great that many players complain that the opportunity to use it occurs so rarely that it has little value. With very powerful hands, though lacking the stated requirements, they make a shaded opening bid of two of a suit. If the partner has a fair share of the outstanding strength, game or even a slam can be made and they congratulate themselves upon the success of their gamble, ignoring the fact that if they had opened with a bid of one of a suit the partner would have made a bid and the same result would probably have been achieved. If, however, the opening two-bid has been shaded and the partner has nothing of value in his hand, there is a very good chance that the opponents will double and will collect a useful penalty.

The requirements for an opening bid of two of a suit have gone up steadily with the years. In the early days of contract bridge five honour tricks in three suits were considered to be sufficient if the trump suit was nearly solid. Later, with normal distribution, it became more than five honour tricks and not more than one trick short of a certain game, even if the partner had a blank hand. And there must be more honour tricks than losers. Counting losers however, was abandoned a few years ago in favour of counting winners and a new formula was introduced. This provided that before opening with a forcing two-bid a player should first count his honour tricks. If the hand contained five or more honour tricks he should then count his winners, but in this count he attaches to his long cards in the trump suit only the same value as long cards in side suits, for at this stage he does not know whether his partner can support the trump suit. If the count of honour tricks added to that of winners adds up to 13 or more, an opening bid of two of a suit may be made. For example with ♠—A.K.10.4.3.2. ♡—A.Q.5. ◇—8.7. ♣—A.K. an opening bid of two of a suit may be made. There are two honour tricks in both spades and clubs, and one and a half in hearts, a total of five and a half. There are the same number of honour trick winners and two long trick winners in spades, a total of seven and a half. The combined total is thirteen, the minimum for an opening two-bid. It is a curious way of valuing the hand, for it will be noticed that the same cards are included in both the honour trick count and the winning honours count, so there is duplication of values, but it works quite well in practice and has been part of the Culbertson system for some years. This hand would also be opened with a two-bid under the older method which many players prefer, of insisting on a minimum of five and a half honour tricks and more honour tricks than losers.

Though five plus honour tricks is a convenient figure for an opening two-bid, it does not follow that holding that strength the bid should be two of a suit and there are occasions when with less than that honour strength an opening bid of two of a suit should be made. Like many other things in bridge it is largely a matter of common sense and good judgment. Every player knows that with freak distribution the honour strength necessary to make a game or even a slam is very much less than that required with a balanced hand. With balanced distribution therefore it is not safe to open with a bid of two of a suit even with five and a half plus honour tricks. Holding ♠—A.Q.7.3. ♡—A.K.6. ◇—A.Q.5.4. ♣—A.7., a hand with six honour tricks, six honour winners and two four card suits counting as one long card winner, though under the rule of thirteen there is a sufficient count to qualify for an opening bid of two of a suit, Mr. Culbertson prefers an opening bid of Two No Trumps. With freak distribution, and only with freak distribution, an opening bid of two of a suit may be made with only four honour tricks. With an eight card suit headed by the two top honours, ace, queen, knave of a second suit and king and another card of a third suit an opening bid of two may be made. With two six card suits headed by the three top honours the forcing two-bid may be used, but the bid is not recommended with 6–5–1–1 or 6–5–2–0 distribution unless the two long suits are practically solid, even with four and a half honour tricks in the hand. One point which should never be forgotten is that the more even the distribution

c

the greater is the honour strength required to make a forcing two-bid. With only four or five cards in the trump suit they should be headed by at least ace, king or king, queen, knave, for it is wise to assume that the outstanding trump strength is held by the opponents. The partner may have some support but it is not safe to assume that he has until he has had an opportunity to bid. Another point to remember is that when an opening forcing to game bid is made, the partner who holds some good cards will visualize slam possibilities immediately. One of the great dangers of shading the requirements for the forcing two-bid is that the partner may take the bit between his teeth and refuse to let the bidding die until the slam zone is reached. A forcing two-bid is always regarded by the partner as an indication that there may be slam possibilities. Not infrequently, however, a player gazing at the picture gallery in his hand feels that there must be game possibilities. The hand falls short of the minimum requirements for a forcing two-bid and his partner having already passed there is a danger that if the bid is only one of a suit it may be left in. With the mental reservation that he will sign off as soon as a game has been bid he makes an opening two-bid. The partner who has a hand on which he had passed on the first round with some reluctance, is not prepared to pay the slightest attention to any attempts which may be made to stop at game and they end in a slam which cannot possibly be made. In view of the fact that an opening bid of two of a suit is usually regarded as an indication of slam possibilities, the opener should be able to guarantee early control of all four suits. If he has only three small cards in any suit, he should try to find some other bid, for it sometimes happens that though the partnership

hands contain enough winning cards to make thirteen tricks, both hands are weak in the same suit and the contract is defeated before the declarer can get in to make his winners. Here is an example :
♠—A.K.Q.J.10.5. ♡—A. ◇—A.K.Q. ♣—7.6.4.
An opening bid of Two Spades is almost certain to lead both partners to consider slam possibilities if the responding hand is ♠—9.8.7.6. ♡—K.Q.J.10.9.7.3.
◇— — ♣—8.3., but though thirteen tricks are certain if a spade, heart or diamond is led the opening lead of a club will defeat a slam contract.

8

RESPONSES TO OPENING TWO-BID

THE opening forcing to game two-bid forces the partner to keep the bidding open even though he has not a card in his hand which is likely to take a trick. With a balanced hand and less than one honour trick he must give the negative response Two No Trumps. With one honour trick and adequate trump support he can raise the opener's suit bid. With one and a half honour tricks and a biddable suit he bids his own suit at the lowest level. With one and a half tricks and no biddable suit or adequate trump support for the opening bid he can show his honour strength by bidding Three No Trumps. If at a later stage the responder bids Four No Trumps he shows that he has two and a half honour tricks at least, while a Five No Trumps bid by the responder shows three honour tricks including one ace. A specialized response to a forcing two-bid is a double raise of the opening bid to show five small trumps or four trumps headed by the queen, with no singleton or void and no honour card higher than a queen in the hand. This response is a weakness warning to kill any slam aspirations in the opener's mind. It is a bid however which should only be made when playing with a good partner. The forcing two-bid is made so seldom that there are many average players who are not very familiar with the specialized bids, and years after he introduced this response Mr. Culbertson admitted that he only made it when he was sure that his partner would understand its meaning. With an

unbalanced hand a suit response to an opening two-bid
may be given with little honour strength if it is in a higher
ranking suit.   Only half an honour trick is necessary to
bid a six card suit or one honour trick to bid a five card
suit.   To make a positive response which raises the
bidding to the three level however, a player should
have one and a half honour tricks.   For some years
we were told to respond by bidding any six card
suit even without any honour strength, but players in
this country thoroughly disliked the bid and it has now
been dropped.   Though it was an aid to reaching the
best game contract, it was too encouraging and frequently
led to the bidding of a slam which could not be made.

Two Club Systems

With Two Club systems the opening forcing to game
bid is Two Clubs.   The strength required for this
bid is much the same as that required by the Culbertson
system.   The Two Club opening forcing bid is preferred
by many players because in the opening stages it keeps
the bidding at the lowest possible level.   It also provides
three other bids, Two Spades, Two Hearts and Two
Diamonds which are strength showing, and hold out a
promise of making game without forcing the partner to
keep the bidding open until game is reached even though
he has a trickless hand.

The Two Club systems have one very great advantage
over the Culbertson system.   The negative response to
a Culbertson forcing two-bid is Two No Trumps, while
in the Two Club systems it is Two Diamonds.   In the
Culbertson system therefore, if the final contract is in no
trumps, it is played with the strong hand on the table,

which may be of considerable advantage to the opponents in planning their defence.

OTHER FORCING BIDS

There are other forcing to game bids which are still more useful, for opportunities to use them occur more often. A player may sit through many rubbers without drawing a hand which is sufficiently strong to justify an opening forcing two-bid, but may much more frequently have sufficient honour strength to make a forcing to game re-bid or a forcing to game bid after his partner's opening bid. Take first the case of the forcing to game re-bid by the player who has opened the bidding. If after opening the bidding with one of a suit and receiving his partner's response, a player wishes to ensure that a game contract shall be reached he will force to game by making a jump re-bid. A jump re-bid is a bid of one trick more than is necessary to keep the bidding open. For example South opens with One Club and North responds with One Heart. South who can now see that there is an almost certain game in the partnership hands for he holds ♠—— ♡—K.J.7.2. ◇—A.Q.5.4. ♣—A.K.J.10.7. bids Three Diamonds which is forcing to game. This is a better bid than Three Hearts, which though strength showing might be passed by North if he had the minimum requirements for a response. A bid of Four Hearts would be open to the objection that it would almost certainly close the bidding and cut out any exploration of slam possibilities. The jump re-bid force is particularly useful when the opener has a strong two suiter. With normal bidding he would open with the higher ranking suit and after his partner's response would bid the other suit. The responder with a moderate hand but liking the lower valued suit better than the suit first bid would be entitled to pass, and probably seeing no prospect of game in a minor suit would let the bidding die. The jump re-bid in the second suit compels him to keep the bidding open until game is reached. After the jump re-bid he has to consider how he can best convey information to his partner about the cards he holds. If he has a second biddable suit he will show it, but it is much more likely that his next bid will be one which shows a preference for one of the two suits bid by his partner.

FORCING BID BY RESPONDER

The forcing to game bid may be made by the responding hand. After an opening bid of one, a jump bid in another suit by the responder is forcing to game. To make this bid the responder should have a considerable amount of strength, for he practically guarantees a game for the partnership if a fit can be found and it is inevitable that the opener, if he has any undisclosed strength will be encouraged to explore slam possibilities. The responder who makes a forcing take out of a suit bid of one should have at least three honour tricks. He must have also either a good biddable suit of his own or strong support for the suit bid by his partner. If he has strong support for his partner's suit a jump bid in that suit would be forcing to game, but the forcing take out may be a better bid because it gives more information about his honour strength. Until he has heard further from his partner who has now taken command, the opening bidder must assume that the responder has a strong biddable suit of his own. But the forcing take out may have been made in an unbiddable lower-ranking suit. North for example may have bid One Spade and South, holding ♠—K.J.7.5.4. ♡—6. ◇—A.7.4.2. ♣—A.K.Q., can see that there is a certain game and possibly a slam in the combined hands. The contract must be to make a certain number of tricks with spades as trumps, but a bid of Three Clubs announcing considerable honour strength may be far better than a bid of Three Spades which could be made on a much weaker hand.

When the opening bid is One No Trump a forcing take out may be made with less honour strength than when the opening bid is one of a suit. The requirements for an opening bid of One No Trump are a minimum of three and a half honour tricks, and a maximum of four defensive honour tricks in at least three suits, with balanced distribution. With a good five card major suit and at least two honour tricks a jump take out may be made. With a seven or eight card major suit, but little honour strength it is better to jump to game than to make a jump take out.

FORCING AFTER OPPONENT'S BID

It is much more difficult to force to game when the opponents have opened the bidding. A jump over bid in another suit shows strength and is strongly invitational to the partner to keep the bidding open, but it is not forcing and the partner is at liberty to pass if he holds a weak hand. The only forcing to game bids open to a defender are an immediate overcall in a suit bid by one of the opponents, or a double of a suit call by one of the opponents, followed on the next round by a jump bid in a new suit by the defender who has doubled. A jump response by the doubler's partner is not forcing, and merely shows a strong biddable suit or a biddable suit in a hand containing about two honour tricks. If South opens the bidding with One Spade and West bids Two Spades, East must keep the bidding open until game is reached. If South bids One Heart, West passes and North bids One Spade, a bid of Two Hearts or Two Spades by East is equally forcing to game. Again if South bids One Spade, West doubles and East bids Two Diamonds, a jump bid of Three Hearts by West is forcing to game. But if South bids One Spade, West doubles and East bids Two Diamonds, a bid of Two Spades by West is not a forcing bid, it is merely a statement that West is prepared to play the hand in a contract with spades as trumps. It is important to remember this difference, for a double of a suit bid followed by a bid of that suit by the doubler, is the best means open to a defender of exposing a psychic bid. The opening bid of One Spade may not have been psychic but may have been a shaded bid by an opponent who has made a light opening bid when not vulnerable, in the hope of making it difficult for his vulnerable opponents to reach a game contract.

ONE ROUND FORCING BIDS

There are hands with which a player is not entitled to force to game but is strong enough to make him anxious to have an opportunity to make a second bid. To meet this situation there are a number of bids which can be made and which are forcing for one round. First of course is the one-over-one response by a player who has not already passed. A one-over-one response or where

.c*

necessary a two-over-one response forces the opener to bid again. This is the most common of the one round forcing bids. A re-bid in a new suit at the level of four if it is not sufficient to produce game is a one round force. A bid in a new suit after a game contract has been reached is also forcing for one round. An overbid in the same suit of a defender's intervening bid, which is sometimes made to show a void or the ace of the suit, is another one round force, for the player making the bid obviously does not desire that the final declaration should be in that suit. This is described as a cue bid and is only made after the partner has bid. It should not be confused with the forcing to game overbid of a suit bid by opponents who have opened the bidding.

9

PRE-EMPTIVE BIDS AND RESPONSES

An opening bid of three of a suit is a very useful bid. It is also one of the most annoying bids in the game. It is reserved for hands containing many playing tricks but not necessarily much honour strength. Its great virtues are that it tells the partner the playing strength of the hand and it makes it difficult for the opponents to intervene, for they have to do so at the range of three or more, and they may lay themselves open to a heavy penalty if the responder is strong enough to double. The opening bid of three of a suit is a limited bid, for it shows great strength in the suit bid and very little outside. The requirements for it when it is made in a major, and when in a minor suit are different. An opening bid of three in a major suit has as its objective a game contract with that suit as trumps, while an opening bid of three in a minor suit invites the responder to bid Three No Trumps if he has stoppers in the other suits. The three-bid is made with a long trump suit of at least six or seven cards and at least seven sure tricks when vulnerable and six when not vulnerable. If the bid is made in a major suit it does not guarantee the top honours in the suit, but if it is made in a minor suit the opener must have two of the three top honours, so that the responder, if he has one of the top honours can count upon making six or seven tricks in the suit if he bids Three No Trumps. Although the bid guarantees six to seven winners if played in the suit bid, a hand on which an opening bid of three is made holds out very little promise of defensive tricks.   One of its main objects is to make bidding difficult for the opponents who may be shut out if they have to open their bidding at the three level.   Third in hand therefore, as the partner has already passed and is not likely to take out a bid of three in a minor suit into no trumps, the condition that the opener must have two of the top honours in his suit may be relaxed, but he must have the playing trick strength required for his bid.

While the opening bid of three is designed largely to prevent the opponents exchanging information without risking a heavy penalty, and is particularly effective when made non-vulnerable against vulnerable opponents, it also to some extent shuts out the partner, who may have a good major suit which he would show at a low level but would hesitate to bid at the range of three.   There are times therefore when with all the requirements for a good opening bid of three, a player should be content to open with a bid of one.   With four cards in one of the major suits and a solid six or seven card minor suit, an opening bid of one is frequently better than a bid of three.

Responses

The strict limits of six to seven winners laid down for an opening bid of three simplify the task of the responder. With less than one and a half honour tricks or three and a half playing tricks he will pass.   With one and a half to three honour tricks in at least two suits he should bid Three No Trumps over a minor suit opening bid of three. There is of course a risk that the opponents may be able to run off enough tricks to defeat the contract in an unguarded suit but the opener may have a guard in that suit. With three and a half distributional or honour winners he may raise a minor suit bid of three, with two and a half winners he may raise a major suit bid of three. To take out from a minor suit the partner should have a strong re-biddable suit and about two and a half honour tricks. To take out an opening three bid in a major suit with a bid of four in a minor suit greater honour strength is required. The responder should have at least three and a half honour tricks.

OPENING BIDS OF FOUR

An opening bid of four of a suit is very similar in its aim and in its promise to an opening bid of three. It is designed to shut out the opponents or, if they refuse to be shut out, to make it difficult to explore the possibilities in the partnership hands without incurring a grave risk of a heavy penalty. Paradoxically, an opening bid of four of a suit, while guaranteeing half a playing trick more than an opening bid of three, is made on a hand with less defensive strength than an opening bid of three. Here the requirements are the same for both major and minor suits. The trump suit has no longer to be solid or nearly solid, so nothing is lost by cutting out the possibility of a response of Three No Trumps. It must however be long, probably about eight or nine cards and capable of taking six tricks. It may have two of the three top honours missing as for example with K.J.10.8.7.5.4.3. or Q.J.10.8.7.5.4.3. The opener guarantees that with his suit as trumps he will probably make eight tricks if not vulnerable, but if he is vulnerable he guarantees that he has eight sure tricks. There is no object to be gained by a response to an opening four-bid in a major suit, unless the partner has so powerful a hand that he wishes to try for a slam, but if the opening four-bid is in a minor suit the responder may raise to five with three honour or ruffing winners.

OPENING BIDS OF FIVE

An opening bid of five in a minor suit is a shut out bid made with a hand which promises nine tricks.

An opening bid of five in a major suit has an entirely different meaning. It guarantees eleven tricks in the hand even if the partner is trickless. It is a slam invitation with a special significance, for it states definitely that the bidder is interested only in missing top honours in the trump suit. With one of the three top honours the partner will raise to six, and with two of them to seven. The responder may have two ace, king suits but unless he has one of the top honours in trumps he must pass the bid of five. The type of hand on which this bid is made is: ♠—Q.J.10.9.8.7.5.3.2. ♡—A.K.Q.J. ◇— — ♣— —.

10

SLAM BIDDING

THE premiums for slams bid and made are large. For a small slam 500 points are awarded above the line if the declarer is not vulnerable and 750 if he is vulnerable, while for a grand slam the premiums are 1,000 when not vulnerable and 1,500 when vulnerable. While the substantial addition to the score which can be secured by the successful bidding of slams is of course the main incentive, there is also the pride of achievement. There are players who obtain even more satisfaction from the successful bidding of a slam than from the premium which it brings them, and if they make a slam without bidding it, there is frequently a prolonged inquest to discover where the partnership failed and how by better bidding they could have reached the right contract.

The bidding of slams being regarded as so important, there have been many devices introduced to assist a partnership to realize that the combined hands are probably in the slam zone. In the early stages of the bidding are the forcing two-bid the forcing re-bid and the forcing take out, which show that with more than average strength in the other hand there are slam possibilities. In the early days of bridge once the trump suit was agreed upon we had the cue bidding of aces, but in later years the majority of bridge players have preferred one or other of the Four No Trump conventions which are now played so widely. The first of these conventions was the Culbertson Four-Five No Trumps Convention which when introduced nearly led to a bridge war with America, for it was denounced in this country as an unfair card showing device. Those who adopted it however found it so useful that the ruling authorities in this country were forced to give way and sanction its use.

THE CULBERTSON FOUR-FIVE NO TRUMP CONVENTION

The Culbertson Four No Trumps bid which is unconditionally forcing for one round asks the partner for information about the aces he holds. It is a condition of the convention that the player bidding Four No Trumps must hold three aces or two aces and the king of a suit bid by either partner. If the responder holds two aces or one ace and the kings of all suits bid by the partnership he must bid Five No Trumps. If holding the ace of an unbid suit or a void, the responder should bid five of that suit though he may sign off if he holds no values not previously shown. If he holds the ace of a bid suit or the kings of all bid suits he should bid six in the best trump suit, provided that he holds values not previously shown. The sign off is the bid of five of the lowest suit bid by the partnership. This bid must be made when the responder does not hold an ace or the kings of all suits bid by the partnership, and should be made even when holding an ace or the kings of all suits bid by the partnership if the hand has no values which have not already been shown.

This convention has been a very valuable aid to slam bidding and, equally important to keeping out of slams which cannot be made. The fact that one of the partners when he has the opportunity does not bid Four No Trumps acts as a warning, for it shows that he has not

got the three aces or two aces and a king of a suit bid, or
that, if he has, his hand is not sufficiently strong to
justify him in slam exploration. The provision that the
responder must sign off if he has no added values, which
means that he has already bid his hand to the limit is
also a safeguard. There are of course hands on which
slam possibilities are evident, but the player desiring to
explore them has not the necessary cards to bid Four No
Trumps. Here more direct methods have to be employed.
North and South for example may hold :

♠—5.4.3.2.
♡—A.Q.J.10.7.
◇—A.Q.
♣—K.3.

```
┌─────────┐
│    N    │
│         │
│         │
│    S    │
└─────────┘
```

♠—A.K.Q.J.7.6.
♡—K.5.
◇—K.J.6.4.
♣—Q.

South opens the bidding with One Spade and North
makes a forcing take out of Three Hearts. It is obvious
to South that if North has the honour strength necessary
to justify his bid, the partnership must be in the slam zone.
North however has taken command and South awaiting
developments bids Three Spades. North now bids

Four Spades being satisfied that if his partner has more than an absolute minimum he will not let the bidding die. South knows that his partner's honour cards must fill most of the blanks in his hand and bids Five Spades. This is a most informative bid for the fact that he does not bid Four No Trumps tells North that he has not two aces and the king of a suit bid by the partnership. How then could he have sufficient strength not merely to open the bidding but to justify his slam try. The suit must be solid and he probably has the kings of hearts and diamonds together with an honour in clubs. North promptly bids Six Spades. This is the correct contract, for though thirteen tricks can be made against any lead but a club, twelve tricks can be made against any lead.

Now let us turn to examples of the position value of the Four No Trumps bid.

♠—K.J.4.3.
♡—Q.J.10.8.7.3.
◇—A.
♣—A.K.

```
┌─────────┐
│    N    │
│         │
│         │
│    S    │
└─────────┘
```

♠—A.Q.7.5.2.
♡—A.K.5.
◇—Q.J.10.
♣—J.7.

South opens the bidding with One Spade and North

makes a forcing bid of Three Hearts. South can make a bid of Four No Trumps at once. This by inference agrees hearts as trumps. When North hears this bid he can place his partner with the ace of spades and the ace and king of hearts. He bids Five No Trumps showing his two aces and South bids Six Hearts. North can count with certainty in the partnership hands two tricks in spades, six in hearts, one in diamonds and two in clubs. His partner has opened the bidding, and after his own response to the opening bid has made an immediate slam try, so must have something beyond the ace of spades and the ace and king of hearts. If he has the queen of spades or the king, queen and another diamond or the king and another diamond and the queen and two small clubs, the grand slam is a certainty, and most players would bid Seven Hearts.

There is sometimes a certain amount of difficulty experienced at the outset in realizing whether the Culbertson Four No Trumps bid is conventional or whether the partner wishes to play the cards in a contract of Four No Trumps. If there has been a strength showing bid by either partner it is definitely conventional. If there has been agreement reached by the partnership about the trump suit it should be regarded as conventional. But if the bidding is North One Spade, South Two Hearts, North Three Diamonds, South Four Clubs, North Four No Trumps, the bid cannot be regarded as conventional. The hands are obviously a misfit and South is entitled to pass, unless it appears to him that the partnership hands are likely to play better in a trump contract.

THE BLACKWOOD CONVENTION

Possibly because players find the strict requirements of

the Culbertson Four-Five No Trumps Convention too restrictive, there has been a great decline in its popularity in recent years. Mr. Culbertson regards it as the most scientific and precise bid in Bridge, but admits that it is costing the players who misuse it millions of pounds a year even at nominal stakes. It is possibly for this reason that a very large proportion of the players in this country have turned over to the Blackwood Convention which is more simple, more precise and less restrictive. Here there is never any doubt whether the Four No Trumps bid is conventional. If either partner has bid a suit and one of the partners subsequently bids Four No Trumps, the bid is conventional. The Blackwood Four No Trumps bid asks the partner to state how many aces he holds. With no ace the response is Five Clubs, with one ace Five Diamonds, with two aces Five Hearts and with three aces Five Spades. A void in the responding hand is ignored in counting aces. If the partner who bids Four No Trumps subsequently bids Five No Trumps he shows that the partnership holds all four aces and asks for a statement of the number of kings held. The response is similar to that to the Four No Trumps bid. With no king the reply is Six Clubs, with one king, Six Diamonds, with two kings Six Hearts, and with three kings, Six Spades. Having heard the response the partner who bid Four No Trumps has to decide whether or not to bid the grand slam. The bid of Five No Trumps when playing rubber bridge is used only as an aid in arriving at a grand slam for it automatically commits the partnership to a small slam. While after the response to a conventional bid of Four No Trumps it is for the maker of the Four No Trumps bid to decide whether or not to bid the small slam, after a subsequent bid of

Five No Trumps, which shows that the partnership holds all four aces, either partner can bid the grand slam. The bidder of Four No Trumps is regarded as the captain of the hand and as such, decides whether a slam should be bid, but there are occasions when he should be over-ruled. If the responder has a void and a good trump suit he has to ignore that void in his reply to the inquiry about the aces he holds. He has values of which his partner has no knowledge and, if the Four No Trumps bidder signs off after hearing his response he is entitled to veto that decision by bidding the slam himself. There are occasions too when a partner with a void will find it unsafe to make the conventional response. If he has one ace and a void, and diamonds are the agreed trumps, a response of Five Diamonds might be passed. He would therefore be justified in ignoring the convention and replying Six Diamonds. This bid would be recognized by his partner as showing one ace and a void, and a fear that if he bid Five Diamonds the bidding might end.

The Blackwood Convention always starts with a bid of Four No Trumps. A player may hold all four aces but he must still bid Four No Trumps. He knows of course that he must receive a response of Five Clubs, but his own subsequent bid of Five No Trumps makes the position clear. In the Blackwood Convention a bid of Five No Trumps not preceded by a bid of Four No Trumps is reserved for a special purpose. It tells the partner that unless his bidding has been shaded a small slam in no trumps can be made and leaves it to him to decide whether to raise to Six No Trumps or to pass.

Playing duplicate bridge with match point scoring it is frequently an advantage to play in a no trump contract rather than in a suit, and one of the disadvantages of the

Blackwood Convention was found to be that if he wished to sign off at the range of five the bidder of Four No Trumps could not do so in no trumps. To meet this difficulty, for duplicate play only, it is provided that if after hearing his partner's response the Four No Trumps bidder makes a bid of five in a hitherto unbid suit, he asks his partner to sign off with a bid of Five No Trumps. Also for duplicate play it is not necessary for a partnership to hold all four aces for a bid of Five No Trumps after a response to a conventional bid of Four No Trumps. Even if there is an ace missing the Five No Trumps bid may be made if it is desired to obtain information about kings before deciding whether to play a small slam in a suit contract or in no trumps.

THE NORMAN CONVENTION

The Culbertson and Blackwood Four No Trumps conventions both had their origin in the United States of America. The Norman Four No Trumps convention which some players consider to be superior to either of the others is British, but possibly because players regard it as more complicated it has never achieved the popularity it deserves. It was invented by the late Sir Norman Bennett and developed by him in collaboration with Mr. Norman de V. Hart. Like the Blackwood it requires no definite holding and can be employed by either partner who has a hand which justifies slam exploration. A bid of Four No Trumps asks the partner to state how many aces and kings he holds. An ace counts one point and a king half a point. With less than one and a half points the response is Five Clubs, with one and a half points which means either one ace and one king or three kings, the response is Five Diamonds, with two points which means two aces,

one ace and two kings, or four kings, the response is Five
Hearts, with two and a half points (one ace and three
kings or two aces and one king) the response is Five
Spades, with three points (two aces and two kings or one
ace and four kings, or three aces), the response is Five No
Trumps. It will be seen that there is a graduated scale
rising with each half point held by the responder. The
great advantage of this system is that after the response to
the Four No Trumps bid, the player who has made the
inquiry is aware of the number of points in the combined
hands and is able to judge whether it is advisable to sign
off at once or whether a slam should be bid. With the
Blackwood Convention, before the number of kings held is
known, the partnership is committed to at least a small
slam. Here is an example of how the Norman Convention works :

♠—Q.10.6.5.2.
♡—A.Q.4.
◇—
♣—K.J.7.4.2.

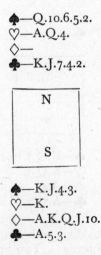

♠—K.J.4.3.
♡—K.
◇—A.K.Q.J.10.
♣—A.5.3.

South is the dealer and bids One Diamond. North responds One Spade. South jumps to Three Spades and when North bids Four Spades, South makes a conventional bid of Four No Trumps. The response of Five Diamonds showing one ace and one king, shows that there is an ace missing. North's king can only be the king of clubs and if his ace is the ace of spades the trump suit should be solid, while if it is the ace of hearts it will provide for a discard of the third club in his own hand. South has no hesitation about bidding Six Spades which North must of course pass.

It is sometimes possible after hearing the response to the Four No Trumps bid to jump to a grand slam with absolute certainty.

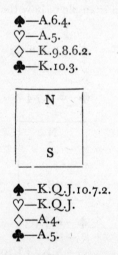

♠—A.6.4.
♡—A.5.
♢—K.9.8.6.2.
♣—K.10.3.

N

S

♠—K.Q.J.10.7.2.
♡—K.Q.J.
♢—A.4.
♣—A.5.

North opens the bidding with One Diamond, South makes a forcing response Two Spades which North raises to Three Spades. South now makes a conventional bid of Four No Trumps and North's response of Five No Trumps shows two aces and two kings. South can see that there are no losers, for the Five No Trumps response has disposed of all his possible losing cards. At rubber bridge he would bid Seven Spades for the sake of the premium for four honours in one hand, but at duplicate bridge with match point scoring at which there are no premiums for honours he would bid Seven No Trumps. If either opponent should be so injudicious as to double he could redouble with confidence, for he knows that there is little possibility of being defeated.

The Grand Slam Force

There is another very useful bid which can be used by a partnership which has reached sufficient agreement as to its strength, to ensure that it is practically certain that a small slam can be made and that there is a strong probability that a grand slam can be bid. The only reason why either partner is likely to refrain from bidding Seven in the agreed trump suit, is that there may be some doubt whether that suit is solid. Each of the partners may have only one of the three top honours in trumps, in which case the grand slam will depend upon a successful finesse, and a grand slam which depends on a finesse should not be bid. To meet this situation, Mr. Culbertson some years ago provided as an optional section of his system, the Grand Slam Force, a bid of Five No Trumps which has not been preceded by a bid of Four No Trumps. This Five No Trumps bid asks one question only, " Have you two of the three top honours in the trump suit ? " With A.K., A.Q., or K.Q. in the trump suit the response is a bid of seven in that suit, while if the responder has not two of the top honours he signs off with a bid of six in the agreed suit. The Grand Slam Force is generally employed after one partner has bid a suit and the other has supported it, but sometimes the suit is agreed by inference. South bids One Spade, North Three Clubs, South Three Hearts, North Five No Trumps, the Grand Slam Force. Here there has been no agreement about trumps and the last suit bid becomes the agreed trump suit. Sometimes the opener after hearing his partner's response knows there may be a grand slam in his partner's suit.

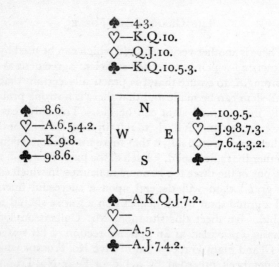

South bids One Spade, West passes and North responds with Two Clubs. After hearing his partner's bid, South knows that there must be a slam and the only question is whether it is a grand slam or a small slam. If North has two of the three top honours in clubs the grand slam should be bid. South accordingly employs the grand slam force of Five No Trumps. North now knows that his partner has taken complete control and that no matter how weak his own hand may be, he must bid Seven Clubs if he has two of the top honours or Six Clubs if he has not got two of the top honours.

GRAND SLAM FORCE VARIATION

The Grand Slam Force is a very useful bid and though in the Culbertson System its use is optional, it is a bid that is widely used both in this country and in the United States. The Americans have introduced a variation of it which can be very effective and is not nearly so complicated as it seems. In order to give additional information in reply to the bid of Five No Trumps, there is a graduated system of responses for the player who has only one of the two top honours. If the agreed trump suit is spades the responder holding the ace or king will bid Six Hearts, with the queen he will bid Six Diamonds and with five trumps without one of the three top honours he will bid Six Clubs. If the agreed trump suit is hearts a bid of Six Diamonds will show the ace or king of hearts, and of Six Clubs will show the queen. If the agreed trump suit is diamonds a bid of Six Clubs will show the ace or king. This variation has much to recommend it, for there are occasions when a player can see that if his partner has one of the top honours, the grand slam can be bid.

11

COMPETITIVE BIDDING

BRIDGE would be a comparatively simple game if it was
not for the opponents who take a fiendish delight in
interfering with the smooth exchange of information.
Intervening bids by the opponents are sometimes helpful
but, particularly when made against timid players, they
may frighten a partnership out of bidding a slam or game,
which could be made. Many books on bridge in showing
how the partnership hands should be bid, dismiss very
briefly, or ignore altogether, the possibility that the opponents may desire to take their share in the auction, and it
comes somewhat as a shock to the novice to discover how
frequently the bidding does not proceed according to
plan. When a player opens the bidding and by so doing
announces that he has a hand which is better than the
average the opponents naturally take notice of the fact,
but it does not and should not stop them from taking part
in the bidding. There are many deals on which both
pairs can bid and make a slam or game, and keen com-
petitive bidding only ends when one of the pairs decide
it will be more profitable to double the opponents for
a penalty than to continue the bidding and incur the
risk that the penalty points will be collected by the
opponents. There was a very interesting example of
this in a duplicate pairs competition at Lederer's Club
some years ago when the late Dr. Paul Stern was the
Tournament Director. The cards were dealt by the
players but some of the boards were placed on a relay

table and Dr. Stern, one of the most remarkable bridge
players the world has seen, quietly substituted a board
prepared beforehand for one which had been dealt:

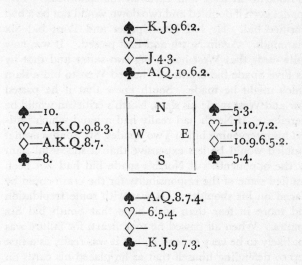

♠—K.J.9.6.2.
♡—
◇—J.4.3.
♣—A.Q.10.6.2.

♠—10.
♡—A.K.Q.9.8.3.
◇—A.K.Q.8.7.
♣—8.

♠—5.3.
♡—J.10.7.2.
◇—10.9.6.5.2.
♣—5.4.

♠—A.Q.8.7.4.
♡—6.5.4.
◇—
♣—K.J.9 7.3.

At one table South passed and West playing the Two
Clubs System bid Two Clubs, which showed the same
strength as an opening two-bid in the Culbertson system.
North, an aggressive player, saw an opportunity for
offensive defence and boldly bid Two Spades. When
East passed, South carried on the good work of making
West's task as difficult as possible by jumping to Four
Spades. West bid Five Hearts, North and East passed.
Five Hearts if made would give a score of 650 points,

for at duplicate bridge 500 points are taken for making a vulnerable game. South reflected that even after an opening forcing to game bid by West, North had put in a bid of Two Spades and must have some strength in addition to at least four cards in the spade suit. Five Spades even if doubled and two down would not be a bad sacrifice bid. He bid Five Spades and West bid Six Diamonds. Again North and East passed. It was now quite clear that West had a big two suiter and that by his Five Spade bid South had helped West to bid a slam which might be made. South knew that if he passed now and West made his slam, North's criticism would be merciless. If North had really had a hand which justified his intervening bid of Two Spades, Six Spades even if doubled would be less expensive than a successful slam by the opponents. If North's spade bid had not been justified some of the responsibility for the crash could be placed on his shoulders. It was with some trepidation and more in fear than with hope that South bid Six Spades. When all passed he took heart, for failure was not likely to be very expensive, but it was really as a first step to defending himself that as he placed his cards on the table he told his partner that he was singularly lacking in courage or he would have bid the grand slam. " Surely," he added, " if I could raise from Two Spades to Six Spades you could bid Seven Spades." To his surprise North, now so meek as to be scarcely recognizable, apologised profusely saying that he had never imagined, after his initial pass, that South could have so strong a hand. Thirteen tricks were of course made, but this was the only table at which the spade slam was bid, the usual contract being Five Hearts doubled.

Not all over-calls by defenders are so successful, but

complete failure may on occasion prove a great success.
Here is an example from duplicate play :

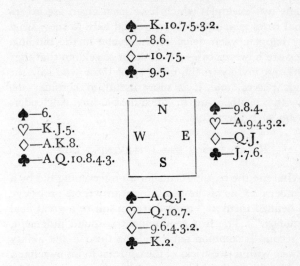

♠—K.10.7.5.3.2.
♡—8.6.
◇—10.7.5.
♣—9.5.

♠—6.
♡—K.J.5.
◇—A.K.8.
♣—A.Q.10.8.4.3.

♠—9.8.4.
♡—A.9.4.3.2.
◇—Q.J.
♣—J.7.6.

♠—A.Q.J.
♡—Q.10.7.
◇—9.6.4.3.2.
♣—K.2.

This board was played at a Congress in the North of
England some years ago. East was the dealer with
East-West vulnerable. At one table West opened the
bidding with One Club and North bid One No Trump
which South, never suspecting that his partner had
interjected a psychic bid, raised to Two No Trumps.
All passed and East led the two of hearts. East-West
took every trick. But for the declarer this was a case of
the more the loss the greater the gain, for though he lost
400 points his opponents could have scored 1430 if they
had bid and made a slam in hearts. At the other table
the contract was Four Hearts, eleven tricks being made

to score 650 points. So though he did not take a single trick the declarer in the Two No Trump contract gained 250 points on the board for his team.

The two examples which have been given are exceptional cases which have been quoted here to show what may happen when defenders intervene in the bidding. They are however cases which occur so seldom that they stand out vividly in the memory of those who saw the hands played, and it is more useful to consider the thousands of other cases in which the bidding of defenders has no such spectacular results.

REQUIREMENTS FOR INTERVENING BIDS

What are the requirements for an intervening bid by a defender ? One of the best American writers on bridge has defined them as " a good trump suit or a great deal of money." The first requirement is sound judgment, the second is common sense and the third is the ability to make within two tricks of the contract in his own hand if vulnerable and within three tricks if not vulnerable. It is one of the anomalies of the game that the average player, with a hand on which he will pass on the first round because he has not the honour strength to make an opening bid, will light-heartedly intervene at the range of two after both opponents have shown strength by bidding and his partner has indicated weakness by passing. That this intervention frequently escapes the heavy punishment it deserves is mainly due to the average player's reluctance to double a low contract, though it is these doubles which frequently produce the best results. On the other hand, against players who are always on the alert for an opportunity for a snap double, it is sometimes good policy to give them a chance to take a small penalty instead of making a game contract. In a duplicate match some years ago one such pair gleefully doubled their opponents on four boards in succession and were very pleased with their achievement until the scores at the two tables were compared and they found that they had lost about 2,000 points on these boards. Gifts by a defender may be a profitable investment. Before a defender decides to intervene in the bidding he should consider first how many tricks he has in his own hand. Even though both opponents have made a bid, his partner may have some cards which may be useful to him though it is always possible that he may have a worthless hand. If he is vulnerable he should be able to count five tricks in his own hand to make a bid at the level of one, while if he is not vulnerable he should have four tricks. Honour strength is not so important as playing tricks strength, and a bid by a defender does not guarantee more than one and a half honour tricks, a good trump suit and the number of playing tricks in the hand which will ensure that the defender will make within two tricks of his contract if vulnerable or three tricks if not vulnerable, even if he receives no help from his partner. This reduction in honour strength for a defender's bid as compared with the strength required for an opening bid is far too widely misunderstood in the early stages of bridge. Over and over again we find weak players attempting to justify light intervening bids on the ground that they had one and a half honour tricks, and entirely disregarding the even more important requirement that they must have a definite number of playing tricks which will limit the loss if they are defeated in a doubled contract. As a general rule it is advisable that there should

D

be at least five cards in the suit bid, and some players insist that there should be not more than two losing tricks in trumps, but a bid may be made on a strong four card trump suit provided that there is sufficient strength in the outside suits to provide the required number of playing tricks.

An over-call by a defender at the range of one is not a strong bid. It is a purely defensive bid, for with a really strong hand the defender could have chosen some other means of telling his partner of his strength. The strongest bid he can make is an immediate over-call in a suit bid by an opponent. This bid is forcing to game and being made after an opponent has shown that he has a hand which is better than the average, shows the type of hand on which, if it had been his turn to open the bidding, the forcing two-bid would have been used or else a hand with freakish distribution. Lacking the requirements for this bid the defender with a good all round hand, at least three honour tricks and no particularly good suit of his own would make an informatory double, asking his partner to bid his best suit or he might bid One No Trump to show much the same type of hand with balanced distribution. With a good suit of his own and a strong hand he could show his strength by a jump bid in that suit. This is frequently a far better bid than a double followed by a bid of his own suit after his partner has disclosed the suit in which his strength may be found. With a hand on which a pre-emptive opening bid of Three would have been made, a double jump to three of his suit should be made and this would be recognized by his partner as showing a hand which will take seven tricks if the partnership is vulnerable and six tricks if they are not vulnerable.

Responses to Over-calls

The responses to over-calls are very simple. If the over-call is made at the range of one, the partner does not get excited. He recognizes it as a defensive call guaranteeing a certain number of tricks with the bidder's suit as trumps. He knows that his partner is depending on him for two of three tricks according to the state of vulnerability. All he has to do is to count up the winners in his own hand and raise the bid once for each winner beyond the number for which his partner has made allowance in his initial calculation. As he is entitled to assume that the over-call has been made on at least a five card suit, he can regard three small cards in the suit or two cards, one of which is one of the three top honours as adequate trump support. With playing trick strength, but lacking trump support he can take out in another suit. If he does so, however, he should have the requirements which applied to his partner's over-call, a strong trump suit of at least five cards and strength sufficient to make his contract if his partner has two or three tricks. Although the first over-call has shown four or five playing tricks with the bidder's suit as trumps, it has not guaranteed more than one and a half honour tricks and the change of trump suit may reduce seriously the number of playing tricks in the hand. There is no obligation on the player making the first over-call to bid again and it follows therefore that if after an over-call the partner sees the possibility of game, he should show the full value of his hand by his response.

Reluctance to intervene when vulnerable, leads to many games being missed. Both sides were vulnerable when South dealt :

<pre>
                    ♠—10.5.
                    ♡—J.10.8.5.3.
                    ♦—
                    ♣—10.9.6.5.4.2.

      ♠—8.7.4.   ┌─────────┐   ♠—Q.9.6.3.
      ♡—A.9.2.   │   N   │   ♡—4.
      ♦—A.J.4.   │ W   E │   ♦—K.Q.9.6.5.2.
      ♣—A.Q.J.3.   │   S   │   ♣—K.8.
                      └─────────┘
                    ♠—A.K.J.2.
                    ♡—K.Q.7.6.
                    ♦—10.8.7.3.
                    ♣—7.
</pre>

South bid One Spade and though West had a hand
which was strong enough for an opening bid he passed.
Neither North nor East felt inclined to take part in the
bidding and South duly made his seven tricks. At the
other table, however, West was more aggressive and
doubled the opening bid of One Spade, to which East
responded with Three No Trumps. South led the ace of
spades which against a no trump contract asked his
partner to play his highest card of the suit. When he
played the ten South switched to another suit to wait for
the spades to be led up to him, but he waited in vain for
the declarer took all the remaining tricks. With a score
of 80 points in one room and 690 in the other there was a
nice swing on this board. The West player who passed
the opening bid of One Spade may have done so hoping
that his opponents would give him the opportunity to
make a profitable double later, but as so often happens

with these trap passes, it was the setter of the trap who was trapped.

Great Britain won the European Bridge Championship for the first time in 1948. They might easily have lost it on the following board dealt by West with East-West vulnerable :

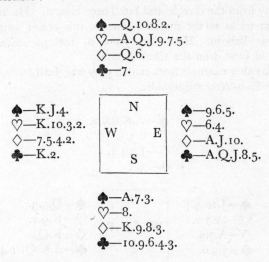

♠—Q.10.8.2.
♡—A.Q.J.9.7.5.
◇—Q.6.
♣—7.

♠—K.J.4.
♡—K.10.3.2.
◇—7.5.4.2.
♣—K.2.

♠—9.6.5.
♡—6.4.
◇—A.J.10.
♣—A.Q.J.8.5.

♠—A.7.3.
♡—8.
◇—K.9.8.3.
♣—10.9.6.4.3.

This was the last board in the match between Great Britain and Iceland. In one room North opened with One Heart, East bid two Clubs, South doubled, and the British North bid Two Hearts, and making eight tricks scored 110 points. In the other room when North bid One Heart, East passed, South bid One No Trump and North Two Hearts. This was not strong bidding and East intervened with a bid of Three Clubs. It may be that he was afraid that he and his partner were missing a possible score, or more likely that these opponents would reach a contract of Three No Trumps and wished to show his partner that he wanted him to lead a club. South doubled, and if the double had been left in, Iceland would have won the match and Great Britain would have lost the Championship. But North ran away from the double and bid Three Hearts. He made eight tricks so the match points on this board went to Great Britain. Had they gone to Iceland, Sweden would have won the Championship.

Another example from match play was dealt by South, with East-West vulnerable.

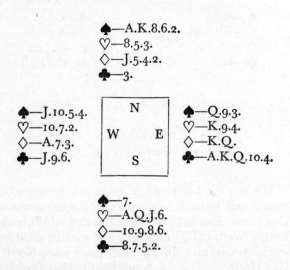

♠—A.K.8.6.2.
♡—8.5.3.
◇—J.5.4.2.
♣—3.

♠—J.10.5.4.
♡—10.7.2.
◇—A.7.3.
♣—J.9.6.

N
W   E
S

♠—Q.9.3.
♡—K.9.4.
◇—K.Q.
♣—A.K.Q.10.4.

♠—7.
♡—A.Q.J.6.
◇—10.9.8.6.
♣—8.7.5.2.

North in both rooms made a light opening bid of One Spade. Obviously he was taking a risk for he had not an opening bid, but it showed some strength and indicated to the partner a safe opening lead. At one table East bid Two Clubs which South Doubled. West, of course, passed, for East's bid of Two Clubs gave no great indication of strength. North could not possibly leave in the double and as the lesser of two evils bid Two Spades. East bid Three Clubs and all passed. At the other table, over the opening bid of One Spade, East showed much greater strength by bidding One No Trump. This completely altered the outlook. South passed and West, who could do nothing over a bid of Two Clubs could take an interest in the bidding. His four spades to the knave, ten assumed trick taking value if his partner had one of the top honours, and with the ace of diamonds and an honour card in each of the other suits he raised his partner to Two No Trumps. East now bid Three Clubs and West Three No Trumps. Ten tricks were made and the swing on the board was 520 points.

12

INFORMATORY DOUBLES

ONE of the most useful weapons of the defenders is the double. When the opponents have opened the bidding a defender, when it is his turn to call, may double. If the double is left in and the declarer makes his contract, the points scored below the line will be doubled and there will be a premium of 50 points above the line. If the contract is Two Spades doubled and the declarer makes eight tricks, his score will be 120 points below the line instead of 60 which would have been made if the contract had been Two Spades not doubled and 50 points above the line for making a doubled contract. This score of 120 will of course, give him game. If the declarer makes more than the eight tricks required by his contract he will score above the line in addition to his premium of 50 points for making his doubled contract, 100 points for each additional trick if he is not vulnerable and 200 points for each additional trick if he is vulnerable. On the other hand if the declarer does not make his contract he will incur a penalty which when not vulnerable is 100 points for the first trick and 200 points for each subsequent trick, and if vulnerable is 200 points for the first trick and 300 points for each subsequent trick. A player who is two down in a doubled contract of Two Spades, incurs a penalty of 300 points when not vulnerable and of 500 points when vulnerable. These penalty points are of course scored by the defenders above the line. When a bid has been doubled, either the declarer or his partner, when it is his turn to bid may redouble, and if the redouble is left in, the score made by the declarer or the penalty points to his opponents, will be twice that which would have been obtained in a doubled contract.

The double however is a two purpose weapon, and its main use is not in fact to produce penalties. While always a strength showing bid, the double is used much more frequently to ask the partner to take out the opponents bid by a bid of his best suit. The informatory or take out double is often the best method of guiding a partnership to the best possible contract, and any player who desires to be successful at bridge should understand it thoroughly. The informatory double is made on a hand containing some strength. As a general rule the doubler should have at least three honour tricks, but three honour tricks alone would not justify a double. The opening bid has shown a hand which should have from at least two and a half to three honour tricks while the informatory double shows three more. There is not very much honour strength in the remaining two hands, and if that strength lies with the left hand opponent, he may redouble. Any bid now made by a defender will probably be doubled and the penalty may be expensive. It may be however, that the partner has some strength. In that case what is he likely to bid ? The player who is considering whether he should double has to bear in mind that the response is quite likely to be the one which he will find most embarrassing. If he gets that response, how will he deal with it ? What is his re-bid over this probable response ? If he has not a sound re-bid it would be better not to double. But if the partner's response

D*

would have been one of the other two suits a possible game might be missed. It is advisable where it can be done without risk to double and thus to announce to the partner that he holds the honour strength which is shown by the bid, for the fact that he does not double will make it difficult for him afterwards to convince his partner that his hand is as strong as it is, but there are occasions when it is better to over-call in a suit than to double the opponent's opening bid. With a very strong two-suiter such as ♠—A.K.Q.9.8. ♡—A.Q.J.10.5. ◇—J.10.7. ♣— —, the hand is much too strong for a double of One Club by the opener. Some players, would bid Two Clubs, an over-bid of the opponent's suit which is forcing to game, for it requires only the ace of diamonds or king of hearts in the partner's hand to give a good chance of making ten tricks with either of the major suits as trumps. More cautious players would make a jump bid in spades, which, without being forcing to game is strongly invitational to the partner to keep the bidding alive if he can find the slightest excuse to do so.

The ideal hand for a take out double is one with a singleton or void in the suit bid by the opponents and good support for a bid by his partner in any of the other suits. South deals and bids One Club. West holds : ♠—K.J.9.8. ♡—A.Q.10.2. ◇—K.Q.7.6. ♣—4. He doubles, and after North has passed, East bids One Spade. When South re-bids his clubs there is a strong temptation to West to bid Four Spades. This however should be resisted. East's bid of One Spade is a forced bid. His hand may be as weak as ♠—7.6.5.4.2. ♡—9.8.7.6. ◇—10.2. ♣—K.7. It is far better to go slowly and to bid Two Spades, for the partner with any strength his hand will not allow the bidding to die. It may be difficult to make even Two Spades if the full deal is :

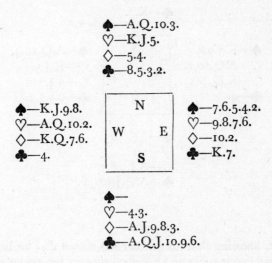

♠—A.Q.10.3.
♡—K.J.5.
◇—5.4.
♣—8.5.3.2.

♠—K.J.9.8.
♡—A.Q.10.2.
◇—K.Q.7.6.
♣—4.

♠—7.6.5.4.2.
♡—9.8.7.6.
◇—10.2.
♣—K.7.

♠—
♡—4.3.
◇—A.J.9.8.3.
♣—A.Q.J.10.9.6.

Though Two Spades can not be made, even if the declarer is doubled, it is not a bad contract for North-South can make Five Clubs against any defence. If the North and

East cards are transposed however, the position is very different.

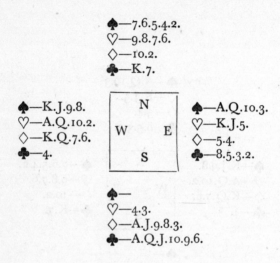

$\spadesuit$—7.6.5.4.2.
$\heartsuit$—9.8.7.6.
$\diamondsuit$—10.2.
$\clubsuit$—K.7.

$\spadesuit$—K.J.9.8.
$\heartsuit$—A.Q.10.2.
$\diamondsuit$—K.Q.7.6.
$\clubsuit$—4.

$\spadesuit$—A.Q.10.3.
$\heartsuit$—K.J.5.
$\diamondsuit$—5.4.
$\clubsuit$—8.5.3.2.

$\spadesuit$—
$\heartsuit$—4.3.
$\diamondsuit$—A.J.9.8.3.
$\clubsuit$—A.Q.J.10.9.6.

East, knowing that his partner has shown that he holds three honour tricks and has good support for spades, can see that there is a possibility of game and tests the situation by bidding Three Spades. West, who has hitherto proceeded cautiously as East's One Spade was a forced bid, can have no hesitation about raising his partner to game. There is nothing in bridge which leads to more acrimonious discussion than does the double. Some players appear to find difficulty in distinguishing between a double which is informatory and demands a take out in the partner's longest suit, and a double which is for a penalty. There is nothing more aggravating than to double for a take out and to hear the partner calmly say " No bid," unless it is to double for a penalty and for the partner to take out the double because he believes that it is meant to be informatory. But the rules governing these doubles are very clear and should be understood thoroughly by every player. A double to be informatory must be a double made by a player at his first opportunity. If he has already said " No bid," and doubles on the second round of bidding, the double is for a penalty. His partner must not have bid though he may have passed. The double must be a double of a suit bid of not more than three. If these necessary requirements are fulfilled, the double is for a take-out and however weak his hand may be, the partner must bid. The only excuse for passing the double would be that the doubler's partner held great strength in the suit bid and could see that it would be more profitable to collect a substantial penalty than for the partnership to play in a contract of their own. When South deals and West doubles, East has no difficulty in recognizing an informatory double, for it is a double made at the first opportunity and must be taken out unless East holds the suit bid by South so strongly that a reasonable penalty seems probable. But if South bids One Spade, West Two Diamonds and after North and East have passed, South doubles, this is still a take out double, which tells the partner that the doubler has good support for any suit he may bid. For this double the first bid must have been an opening bid of one of a suit. The strength required to take out an opponent's suit bid of one with an informatory double, is three honour tricks in three suits or three honour tricks in two suits one of which should be a rebiddable suit with four trump tricks. An informatory double of a major suit bid of one, usually implies support for the other major suit. A player is frequently presented with the problem, whether to make a simple or jump overcall in a strong suit of his own or to make an informatory double. The double may be the better bid, for it tells the partner at once about the honour strength of the hand. With a very strong hand, a better bid may be an immediate over-call in the opponent's suit which is the only bid forcing to game when the opponents open the bidding. A double of an opening bid of One No Trump is not an informatory double, it is a double for penalties and should be left in.

Responses to Informatory Doubles

There are few more embarrassing moments at the bridge table than when a player is faced with the realization that an opponent has opened the bidding, partner has made an informatory double and a take out has to be made on a hand which has not even the most remote prospect of taking a single trick. The opening bid has been One Spade and the doubler's partner holds ♠—7.6.4.3. ♡—5.4.2. ♢8.7.5. ♣—4.3.2. It is on an occasion of this kind that a player develops an intense dislike for his partner. Had any other suit been bid, his normal response would have been One Spade to show his partner his best suit. It would have been a poor best but it would at any rate have shown his longest suit. He must make some bid, for the one thing which he cannot do is to pass. His best response is to bid Two Clubs, which will enable the doubler to bid his own suit at the lowest possible level. With a completely worthless hand, even with four cards in the other major suit, it is better to bid the lowest three card minor rather than a four card major if the response has to be made at the range of two. If the hand contains from one half to one plus honour tricks it is better to bid a four card major suit than a five card minor suit, provided that the major suit contains one of the four top honours, for a take out double implies some strength in the major suits. If the bid doubled has been one of the major suits, the partner is likely to have strength in the other. If he has not he must have a good suit of his own. With only half an honour trick and two four card major suits the lower ranking suit should be bid first to give the doubler a chance to bid the other without increasing the number of tricks to be made, but with greater honour strength the higher ranking suit should be bid first even though it is the weaker suit. With one and a half to two honour tricks and no five card suit or strong four card suit a response of One No Trump may be made even without a stopper in the opponent's suit. A stopper in the suit can be shown on the next round by repeating the no trump bid over the suit bid made by the doubler. A response of Two No Trumps to the double of one of a suit shows two honour tricks and two probable stoppers in the opponent's suit. While as a general rule when holding a strong hand on the left of an opening bid it is better to bid a long suit than to double, to ask the partner to bid his best suit, freakish distribution can upset all calculations. Here is an instance from an international match. North was the dealer with North-South vulnerable and he opened the bidding with One Club. East held : ♠—A.Q.9.6.4.3. ♡—A.K.10.4.3. ◇—10.

♣—J. With a strong two-suiter hand he felt that if his partner could support either of his suits there was a good possibility of game so bid One Spade, intending to show the heart suit on the second round. But South bid Two Hearts. Obviously this meant that he had either four hearts headed by queen, knave, or five with one honour, for a vulnerable player was not likely to bid the suit with less. East's trick possibilities in the heart suit were now not so promising. West bid Two Spades and North Three Hearts. East now knows that his partner has some help in spades, probably three headed by the king. On the bidding he cannot have more than one heart, for the suit has been bid by South and supported by North, and it is quite possible that he may have playing tricks in the minor suits. East bid Four Spades and was satisfied that the partnership had done well when he made ten tricks and a score of 420 points. The full deal was :

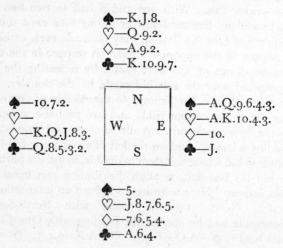

North
♠—K.J.8.
♡—Q.9.2.
◇—A.9.2.
♣—K.10.9.7.

West
♠—10.7.2.
♡—
◇—K.Q.J.8.3.
♣—Q.8.5.3.2.

East
♠—A.Q.9.6.4.3.
♡—A.K.10.4.3.
◇—10.
♣—J.

South
♠—5.
♡—J.8.7.6.5.
◇—7.6.5.4.
♣—A.6.4.

Looking at the four hands it will be seen that had East doubled the opening bid of One Club, West would have bid One Diamond, and as he had not bid his six card major suit at once, East might have found it very difficult to reach a contract of Four Spades. At the other table, however, East preferred to double rather than bid his spades. South bid Two Clubs which East doubled and the penalty was 1100 points, for the declarer only made four tricks.

13

PENALTY DOUBLES

To double for a penalty is attractive, particularly when the opponents are vulnerable, for if the contract can be defeated by two tricks the penalty is 500 points. But sound judgment is required, for an unsuccessful double may present the declarer with a game which he could not have made, or the doubler may be sacrificing a game or even a slam which he and his partner could have made in order to obtain a small penalty. Psychology and knowledge of the opponents may be a deciding factor in considering whether or not to double. Many players are necessarily confined to a small circle in which they become well acquainted with the views and characteristics of all the other players. If the opponents are known to be forward bidders prepared to take risks, it may be much more profitable to double than to make an overcall, while if they are notoriously under-bidders a double is not likely to prove profitable.

Many players are most reluctant to double a low contract but without hesitation will step in with a double when the opponents have reached the game or slam level. Many of the most profitable doubles are those of low contracts for, in bidding at the range of one or two tricks, much less is known of the position of the outstanding cards and consequently more risks are run. Good players rarely bid up to a slam contract unless there is a reasonable chance of making it, and a double of a slam, unless it is a lead directing double, or the bidding of a slam is a sacrifice bid, is not a sound gambling proposition. For the sake of an additional 50 points if the opponents are not vulnerable, or 100 points if they are vulnerable, the doubler is offering them an additional 230 points if the contract is in a major suit, or 170 points if it is in a minor suit. If the declarer or his partner re-doubles and the contract is made, the declarer will score 720 below the line plus 50 points premium if the slam is in a major suit or 480 points below the line plus 50 points premium if it is in a minor suit, instead of 180 or 120 below the line if the contract is not doubled.

Freakish distribution can upset what appears to be an absolute certainty. In a duplicate competition, West must have felt that the opponents had gone mad when they bid up to Six Diamonds and she looked at the picture gallery in her own hand : ♠—K.Q.J.10 ♡—K.Q.J.9. ◇—Q.J. ♣—K.Q.8. Few players could resist a double and even when the opponents redoubled she could have had no qualms. But the full deal was :

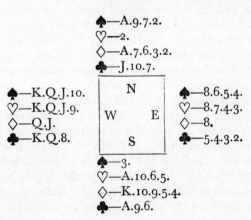

By drawing trumps, ruffing out spades and hearts and leading the knave of clubs up to West's K.Q.8. at the eleventh trick, the declarer had no difficulty in making his redoubled contract in spite of West's array of honour cards. The failure of the double in this instance is not intended as a warning against doubling, but merely as an indication that caution should be exercised if there is reason to suspect freak distribution.

In deciding whether to double or to make a try for game a player should have some regard to the position with regard to vulnerability. If the opponents are vulnerable it would be more profitable to get them down two or three tricks than to score a non-vulnerable game, but if the doubling side is vulnerable it may pay better to go for game and rubber than to obtain only a small penalty by doubling non-vulnerable opponents. When facing opponents who are known to be hair-trigger doublers, it is sometimes good policy to make an over call with a long, fairly solid suit and little outside it rather than to pass and let the opponents reach a game contract they are likely to make. There are some players who cannot resist the bait, and it has a depressing effect on partnership confidence if the double brings in only a penalty of 100 points when a game could have been made and 700 points scored for the rubber.

While there should be at least three honour tricks in the hand to make a penalty double, less strength is required after the partner has opened the bidding and an opponent has over-called in a suit. If North has opened One No Trump and East has bid Two Clubs South, holding ♠—K.7. ♡—Q.6.2. ◇—J.10.8.7. ♣—K.J.10.5., can either double or bid Two No Trumps. If the opponents are vulnerable and he and his partner are not, the double of Two Clubs may be the better choice. His partner's One No Trump has shown a balanced hand with three and a half honour tricks and even with freakish distribution there should be a penalty of 500 or 800 points. Sometimes a double is used as the instrument with which to close the partner's mouth. North deals and passes, East bids One Heart and South, vulnerable, makes an over call of One Spade on a hand which only just satisfies the requirements for an over-call. West bids One No Trump and North jumps to Three Spades. When East bids Four Hearts, South doubles, not because he thinks the contract can be defeated, but because he fears that without the double North will bid Four Spades, and Four Spades doubled may be much more expensive than to allow East to play in a doubled contract of Four Hearts, which he may make.

14

THE PLAY OF THE CARDS

WHILE sound bidding is a most important factor in the game of bridge, the ability to play the cards well is essential to success. It is a very heavy handicap if a player is sufficiently skilful to bid his cards accurately enough to secure that the best contract is reached, but is so poor a player of the cards that he cannot make all the tricks which are there. Good card play so largely influences the result that a good card player drawing poor hands can reduce his losses to the minimum when acting on the defensive, while when he is the declarer he can frequently make a difficult contract which would completely baffle an inferior player.

Let us consider first the play of the cards by the declarer. He has a great advantage over his opponents for, while all three players can see 26 cards after dummy's hand has been placed on the table, he alone knows definitely what is the composition of the partnership hands. All three players can make certain deductions from the bidding which will enable them to place certain cards in the hands of the other players, but only the declarer knows definitely the complete fit or misfit of the partnership hands. When the opponent on his left has made the opening lead and dummy's cards have been placed on the table, it is the duty of the declarer to survey the position very carefully in the light of all the information he has now and to draw up his plan of campaign in order to give himself the best chance to make his contract.   That plan may have to be changed as play proceeds and more information is acquired and it is only by constant alertness and sound judgment that the declarer in a difficult contract can succeed.   There are occasions of course when the declarer can make his contract by accident, as for example, when on one occasion, forced by his partner into an impossible contract of Six Diamonds, in a moment of mental aberration he imagined that he was playing the cards in no trumps, led out his long string of diamonds and made his contract by squeezing both opponents when his only object had been to make as many tricks as possible before the opponents got in to make their good cards.   But cases of this kind are so rare that they can be disregarded and as a general rule it is planning which ensures success when the declarer finds himself in a difficult contract.

Here is a deal which called for careful consideration :

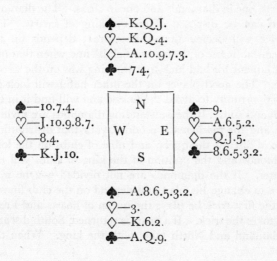

♠—K.Q.J.
♡—K.Q.4.
◇—A.10.9.7.3.
♣—7.4.

♠—10.7.4.
♡—J.10.9.8.7.
◇—8.4.
♣—K.J.10.

N
W   E
S

♠—9.
♡—A.6.5.2.
◇—Q.J.5.
♣—8.6.5.3.2.

♠—A.8.6.5.3.2.
♡—3.
◇—K.6.2.
♣—A.Q.9.

South is the declarer in a contract of Six Spades and when West leads the knave of hearts and dummy's hand goes down, the declarer must survey the position and draw up his plan. He is entitled to take time to consider how the hand should be played, and he should not hesitate to do so. Prolonged consideration however, should, if possible, be avoided for it is a warning to the opponents that he may be in difficulties and encourages them to exercise special alertness. On this deal there has been no opposition bidding so there is nothing to be learned about the composition of the defenders' hands. The declarer can count six tricks in trumps and a possible seventh if the outstanding trumps are divided equally and he can ruff a club in dummy. He has one trick in hearts, two in diamonds and one, possibly two tricks in clubs if the finesse of the queen succeeds. Looking at the hands another way he can see three possible losers—one in hearts, one in diamonds and one in clubs. The diamond loser can be disposed of on the king of hearts. The novice will decide that the contract depends on the successful finesse of the queen of clubs, and when that fails will lament his bad luck that the king was on the wrong side. The good player on the other hand will look for an opportunity to avoid the finesse and will find it in the diamond suit. If the outstanding diamonds are divided 3–2 and the mathematical odds favour that distribution, he can discard the queen and nine of clubs on the long diamonds and the position of the king of clubs will not matter. If the diamonds are not divided 3–2 he may have to change his plan and depend on the club finesse. At the first trick he plays the queen of hearts and East's ace takes the trick. If a heart is returned, South discards a diamond and North takes with the king. When the hand was played, East led a trump which was taken by North's knave though a better lead would have been a club, which would have set the declarer immediately the problem of taking the club finesse. When West played in on the lead of a trump the declarer felt that he had cleared his first obstacle. The king of hearts was made, South discarding a diamond. The king and ace of diamonds made the next two tricks and when both opponents followed suit on the second round the contract was safe. A third diamond was ruffed with the ace and a trump was led to North's queen. The king of trumps followed, drawing West's last trump, and North made two tricks in diamonds on which the declarer discarded his losing clubs.

DEDUCTIONS FROM THE BIDDING

Sometimes the declarer has much more information than he had on the last deal.

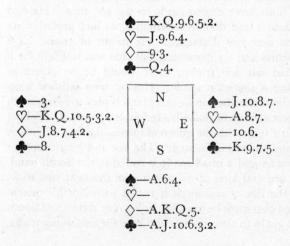

♠—K.Q.9.6.5.2.
♡—J.9.6.4.
◇—9.3.
♣—Q.4.

♠—3.
♡—K.Q.10.5.3.2.
◇—J.8.7.4.2.
♣—8.

♠—J.10.8.7.
♡—A.8.7.
◇—10.6.
♣—K.9.7.5.

♠—A.6.4.
♡—
◇—A.K.Q.5.
♣—A.J.10.6.3.2.

South was the dealer with neither side vulnerable. South opened with One Club, West bid One Heart, North One Spade, East One No Trump, South Two Hearts, a very strong bid showing first round control of the suit, North Two Spades, East Three Hearts, South Four Diamonds, West Double, North Five Clubs. South Six Clubs, East Double, South Redouble. West led the three of spades. When North's hand went down and the declarer made his survey, he reviewed the bidding. West had bid One Heart and doubled Four Diamonds. East had bid One No Trump over North's One Spade and his own bid of One Club. He had also supported his partner's heart bid and had doubled Six Clubs. If the One No Trump bid was sound, East must hold four spades to the knave and probably four clubs to the king, while his support of hearts showed three cards in the suit. If these deductions about East's hand were sound then West could only have one spade and one club and must have eleven cards in the red suits. He had bid hearts and doubled diamonds, so had probably six hearts and five diamonds. He might of course have six hearts and six diamonds, but that was unlikely for if he had not one trump, there would be no object in leading a singleton spade. Having now satisfied himself about distribution he can plan his play to give himself his best chance to make his redoubled contract. Taking the first trick with the queen of spades, the four of clubs is led and the ten is finessed. The ace and king of spades are made and a small spade is ruffed in the South hand. The ace and king of diamonds take the next two tricks and the five of diamonds is ruffed with North's queen. If East over-ruffs he must lead a heart or a club and South must get in to clear trumps and take the remaining tricks .

East's best play is to refuse to over-ruff and North leads a spade, East discards a heart and South the queen of diamonds. Another spade is led on which East discards the ace of hearts. South has nothing left but trumps so ruffs and leads a small trump to put East in to lead from the king, nine of clubs up to South's ace, knave.

Sometimes it is merely a case of keeping alert and drawing deductions from the cards played. Here is a type of deal on which the declarer's problem may appear difficult at first, but to which on very little reflection there is an obvious solution.

♠—Q.8.2.
♡—A.K.J.2.
◇—J.3.2.
♣—5.3.2.

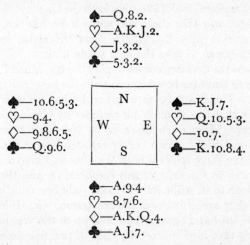

♠—10.6.5.3.
♡—9.4.
◇—9.8.6.5.
♣—Q.9.6.

♠—K.J.7.
♡—Q.10.5.3.
◇—10.7.
♣—K.10.8.4.

♠—A.9.4.
♡—8.7.6.
◇—A.K.Q.4.
♣—A.J.7.

South is the declarer in a contract of Three No Trumps and West leads the three of spades. When North's hand goes down the declarer can see eight tricks and to make his contract, one trick will have to be developed in play. There is a possibility in the finesse against the queen of hearts, while if that fails a 4-3-3-3 division of hearts or diamonds may enable a trick to be made with the long card of the suit. His review completed, the declarer plays the two of spades from dummy's hand. East plays the knave and South takes with the ace. To an alert declarer the ninth trick is no longer a problem. The play of the knave of spades by East is a clear indication that East does not hold the ten, unless the knave was a false card and it is most unlikely that East would false card on his partner's opening lead. The ten, therefore, can be placed with West so the declarer can lead the four up to North's queen, eight. If West plays low the eight is finessed, and if West has both the king and the ten, the eight will take the trick, while if he has not, East will have to play the king to beat the eight, leaving North's queen to take the next spade trick.

When the declarer comes to play the combined hands, he has to consider how he can attain the best results with them. There will be times when he has no worry, he can see that he can make his contract by playing out his winners. More often however he will have to set up additional tricks. With ace, queen, ten in one hand, he can make three tricks if both the king and knave are in the hand on the right of this combination and the lead comes up to it, while he will make only one trick in the suit if they are sitting over the ace, queen, ten. If he can get the left hand opponent to lead up to the ace, queen, ten, his task is of course easy, but in practice defenders will rarely be so obliging. He will generally find that he has to develop his tricks himself in which case he will assume that the two important missing cards are where he would like them to be, and will lead from the other hand up to the ace, queen, ten and finesse the ten. Entering the other hand again, he will lead the suit a second time and finesse the queen. If the combination is ace, knave, ten, the same principle is followed and when the king and queen are in different hands, this play will produce two tricks. If the declarer holds king, queen, seven of a suit, he can make two tricks if the ace is on his right by leading up to the suit from dummy, but he can only make one trick if he leads away from these cards. Again with ace, seven, six in one hand and queen, five, two in the other, the declarer can make two tricks if he plays out the ace and leads up to the queen when the king is on the queen's right. It is an even chance which opponent holds the king and if it is in the hand over the queen, only one trick can be made. If the declarer has to open the suit himself this line of play gives him the best chance to make two tricks in the suit. There will be times when from the bidding, the declarer can deduce that the king is in the hand over the queen, but even then it may be possible to make both the ace and the queen by playing out the other suits and throwing in the player holding the king to lead away from it.

The declarer is frequently faced with a difficult decision when he has ace, king, knave of a suit and the combined hands contain the larger proportion of cards in the suit. If he finesses the knave and the trick is taken by the queen, he may find that he has lost a trick he could have made for by playing out the ace and king he would have dropped the queen. The rule which is generally followed with this combination is that with nine cards of the suit in the partnership hands, an even distribution of the four outstanding cards is assumed and the ace and king are led out. With fewer than nine cards in the two hands one of the opponents must have three cards in the suit and the queen is more likely to be in the hand with three cards, than in the hand with only two, so the knave is finessed. With eleven cards in the two hands headed by the ace, queen the ace is played in the hope of dropping the king, with fewer than eleven cards the finesse is taken, for one of the opponents must have more than one card of the suit, and the assumption is that he will hold the king. Working on these lines the declarer with A.Q.10.7.4. of a suit in one hand will consider how he should play. If he has four cards of the suit in the other hand he will assume that the outstanding cards are evenly divided and will finesse the queen on the first round, hoping that if this is successful the play of the ace will drop the king. If he has only eight cards in the combined hands he will know that one of his opponents has at least three cards of the suit and will finesse the ten on the first round.

SACRIFICING A TRICK

Very often the declarer will be called upon to sacrifice a trick which he could have made. Playing in a no trump contract he finds dummy holds A.K.Q.7.5.2. of a suit and no re-entry card. He has the six and four in his own hand, so there are five cards in the suit in the hands of the defenders. The mathematical odds are very much in favour of a 3–2 distribution, but if the declarer can afford to lose one trick in the suit, he should allow his opponents to take the first trick. This will guard against a 4–1 division which would confine him to three tricks in the suit. Even though he finds that by leading out the ace, king and queen he would have cleared the suit there will be ample compensation for the occasional loss of a trick when there is a 4–1 division of the cards and by this safety play he is able to make five tricks in the suit instead of only three.

When playing in a no trump contract it is frequently necessary for the declarer to sacrifice possible winning cards. South is playing in a contract of Three No Trumps and West leads the seven of a suit up to king, queen, five in the declarer's hand, East plays the ten and though he could take the trick with the queen the declarer allows East to make his ten. This will sacrifice a trick if West gets in and leads the suit again, but it is a necessary precaution, for should East obtain the lead and return his partner's suit up to the ace knave of the suit the declarer will probably lose four or five tricks at once if he has played the queen at the first trick. By ducking the first trick he ensures that part of the danger is removed, for though East leads the suit back, unless West has an outside entry card, by the time the long cards are established, they will be useless for East cannot put his partner in to make them. The following deal shows clearly the advantage to the declarer of this hold-up play :

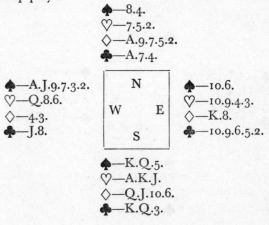

♠—8.4.
♡—7.5.2.
◇—A.9.7.5.2.
♣—A.7.4.

♠—A.J.9.7.3.2.
♡—Q.8.6.
◇—4.3.
♣—J.8.

N
W E
S

♠—10.6.
♡—10.9.4.3.
◇—K.8.
♣—10.9.6.5.2.

♠—K.Q.5.
♡—A.K.J.
◇—Q.J.10.6.
♣—K.Q.3.

It will be seen that when the seven of spades is led and East plays the ten, if South takes with the queen he must start on the diamond suit and lose a trick to East who will lead the six of spades. By ducking the first trick, the declarer ensures that when East gets in with the king of diamonds he has no spade to lead.

Hold up play is one of the first things the declarer should consider when he is in a no trump contract, but the hold up on the first trick should not be regarded as the correct play in all circumstances for there are times when it is entirely unnecessary. If the declarer can see that it is likely that he will be able to keep East out of the lead for he can take all his finesses into the West hand, to duck on the first round would mean the unnecessary loss of a trick. If the hands in the last deal are altered slightly, a different line of play should be followed.

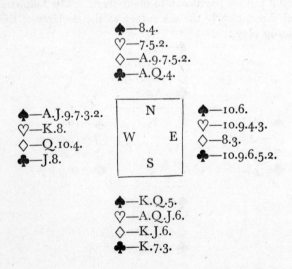

```
                    ♠—8.4.
                    ♡—7.5.2.
                    ◇—A.9.7.5.2.
                    ♣—A.Q.4.

♠—A.J.9.7.3.2.        ┌─────────┐        ♠—10.6.
♡—K.8.                │    N    │        ♡—10.9.4.3.
◇—Q.10.4.             │ W     E │        ◇—8.3.
♣—J.8.                │    S    │        ♣—10.9.6.5.2.
                      └─────────┘

                    ♠—K.Q.5.
                    ♡—A.Q.J.6.
                    ◇—K.J.6.
                    ♣—K.7.3.
```

Here the declarer can take the first trick with confidence for he can see that there is no danger of East getting in to lead a spade through South's hand as the finesse in diamonds can be taken into West's hand and if it fails the lead of another spade will do no harm. On taking the first trick with the queen he enters dummy with the queen of clubs and leads the two of diamonds finessing the knave. West takes with the queen and whatever he leads the contract is safe.

15

ELIMINATION PLAY

ELIMINATION play may enable a declarer to make his contract, when any other line of play would fail. Elimination play is an end play which consists of stripping the opponents of their cards in the other suits then throwing the lead to a defender who must lead up to a tenace in the hand of one of his opponents, or perhaps lead a suit which will enable the declarer to ruff in one hand and discard from the other. Here is an example :

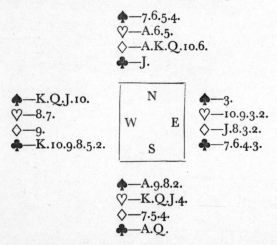

♠—7.6.5.4.
♡—A.6.5.
◇—A.K.Q.10.6.
♣—J.

♠—K.Q.J.10.
♡—8.7.
◇—9.
♣—K.10.9.8.5.2.

♠—3.
♡—10.9.3.2.
◇—J.8.3.2.
♣—7.6.4.3.

♠—A.9.8.2.
♡—K.Q.J.4.
◇—7.5.4.
♣—A.Q.

South is the declarer in a contract of Four No Trumps and West leads the king of spades, after having opened the bidding with One Club. The declarer reviewing the partnership hands can count one trick in spades, four in hearts, at least three in diamonds and one, possibly two in clubs, though on the bidding it is unlikely that the club finesse will be successful. He ducks the first trick and when the queen follows and East plays out he knows that West held originally four honours in spades. The ace is played and the first thing is to test the diamond situation. West discards a club on the second round of diamonds. Four rounds of hearts are taken and when West discards on the third round the declarer knows that he held originally ten cards in the black suits, six in clubs and four in spades. After making his winners in the red suits the declarer throws West in with a spade, and after taking two tricks in the suit, West has to lead from the king, ten to South's ace, queen of clubs.

When there is a trump suit, elimination play is sometimes more easy, for there is the additional chance of forcing a ruff-discard as in the following deal :

♠—A.10.5.4.
♡—8.7.6.
◇—K.5.2.
♣—A.10.9.

♠—9.3.2.   ♠—8.6.
♡—A.K.3.2.   ♡—9.5.4.
◇—9.8.6.   ◇—Q.J.10.7.
♣—Q.8.6.   ♣—5.4.3.2.

	N	
W		E
	S	

♠—K.Q.J.7.
♡—Q.J.10.
◇—A.4.3.
♣—K.J.7.

South is the declarer in a contract of Four Spades and when West leads the king of hearts he can see four tricks in spades, one in hearts, two in diamonds and two in clubs. The tenth trick appears to depend on guessing correctly which of the defenders holds the queen of clubs and he can take the finesse either way. There is however no need to run any risk, he can let the defenders solve his problem for him. He gets in at the third trick with the queen of hearts and plays out three rounds of trumps, clearing the suit followed by three rounds of diamonds, the last of which is taken by East, who is left with the last diamond and three small clubs. If he leads a diamond, South ruffs and North discards the nine of clubs which enables him to ruff the third round of clubs. If East leads a club, West's queen is trapped and North-South make three club tricks.

The defenders are of course fully alive to the danger of being end-played and in order to avoid falling into the declarer's trap they occasionally get rid of a high card to enable the partner to obtain the lead at the critical trick. What is probably the most spectacular example of this occurred in London Club play some years ago on the following deal :

♠—A.K.Q.
♡—K.5.
◇—6.5.3.2.
♣—8.7.5.3.

♠—J.9.8.7.6.5.4.3.2.   ♠—10.
♡—   ♡—A.Q.9.7.6.4.3.2.
◇—K.4.   ◇—8.
♣—9.6.   ♣—10.4.2.

```
       N
  W         E
       S
```

♠—
♡—J.10.8.
◇—A.Q.J.10.9.7.
♣—A.K.Q.J.

West opened the bidding with Four Spades. North doubled and South bid Six Diamonds. The nine of clubs was led, taken by the knave, and South played out the ace of diamonds. West realizing that the declarer was void of spades saw the danger of being thrown in with only spades to lead so played his king of trumps under the ace. Had he not done so another round of clubs would have left him with only the king of diamonds and nine spades, and a diamond lead would have given him the lead with nothing but spades in his hand. By giving up a certain trick in trumps, West at the second trick avoided an " end-play " and enabled his partner to defeat the contract with his ace and queen of hearts, for the declarer could not put North in to make his spade tricks.

An end-play which is not unusual is employed when the

declarer finds or has reason to suspect that both the king and queen of a suit, usually trumps, are in the hand sitting over the ace and he can only afford to lose one trick :

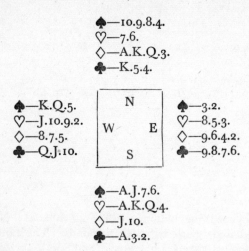

♠—10.9.8.4.
♡—7.6.
◇—A.K.Q.3.
♣—K.5.4.

♠—K.Q.5.
♡—J.10.9.2.
◇—8.7.5.
♣—Q.J.10.

♠—3.2.
♡—8.5.3.
◇—9.6.4.2.
♣—9.8.7.6.

♠—A.J.7.6.
♡—A.K.Q.4.
◇—J.10.
♣—A.3.2.

South is playing in a contract of Six Spades which West has doubled and the queen of clubs is led. When the declarer studies the hands he can see that if West has not merely doubled on hope, he must have done so on the strength of holding the king and queen of spades sitting over the declarer's ace. That being so there is only one chance of making the contract. He must play out his winners in the side suits and hope that West will be able to follow suit and that he has only three trumps. He takes the first trick with the ace of clubs in his own hand and makes dummy's ace, king and queen of diamonds, discarding a club from his own hand. The king of clubs is led and a club is ruffed. South now leads out the ace,

king and queen of hearts followed by the four which
North ruffs with the eight. The ten of trumps is led and
run up to West's king, queen, five. West must take and
lead from king, five for the declarer to make the last two
tricks and his contract.

SQUEEZE PLAY

Although it is much too difficult for the beginner at
bridge to master, he should know something of the possibilities of squeeze play. The squeeze is usually the
work of the declarer who, to set up an extra trick in his
own hand or dummy's, leads out his winners until one or
both of the defenders discard a winning card. It is an
end play which when thoroughly understood is worth
many thousands of points in the course of a year, but a
very large proportion of average players regard the play
as so complex that they never devote sufficient time and
trouble to learning all they can about it. An elementary
example of the squeeze is :

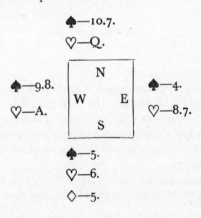

Here when South leads the five of diamonds, West must discard a spade or a heart. If he discards a spade, North discards a heart, while if he discards a heart, North discards a spade.

Sometimes the squeeze affects both opponents.

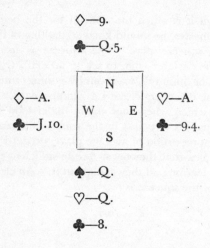

When South leads the queen of spades, West is squeezed in diamonds and clubs. He will probably discard a club and North will play the nine of diamonds. East cannot discard a club without giving North two tricks in the suit, while if he discards the ace of hearts South will make the queen.

These squeezes are simple when the cards have been reduced to three or four in each hand, but they are much more difficult when the end play has to be foreseen, possibly at the first trick and the declarer has to plan his play to produce the required squeeze position.

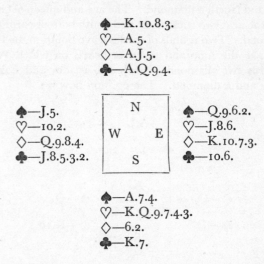

♠—K.10.8.3.
♡—A.5.
◇—A.J.5.
♣—A.Q.9.4.

♠—J.5.
♡—10.2.
◇—Q.9.8.4.
♣—J.8.5.3.2.

♠—Q.9.6.2.
♡—J.8.6.
◇—K.10.7.3.
♣—10.6.

♠—A.7.4.
♡—K.Q.9.7.4.3.
◇—6.2.
♣—K.7.

The contract is Seven Hearts by South and West leads the ten of trumps. South can count two tricks in spades, probably six in hearts, one in diamonds and three in clubs. How is he going to make his 13th trick? If the outstanding spades are evenly divided it may be possible, by discarding a spade from the South hand on the third round of clubs and then ruffing the third round of spades, to establish North's fourth spade. The mathematical probabilities are however much more in favour of 4–2 than of 3–3 distribution of the outstanding spades, and there appears to be a much better chance of making 13 tricks by squeezing the opponents. Two rounds of trumps are taken and the king of clubs is made. A third round of trumps draws East's knave, West discarding a club and North a diamond. The ace and queen of clubs take the next two tricks, East and South both discarding a diamond. Two rounds of spades leave South in the lead to make the nine and seven of hearts on which West discards two diamonds, North two spades and East a spade and a diamond. The position now is :

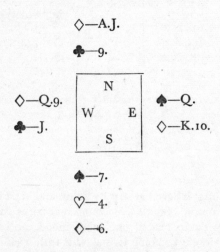

When South leads the four of hearts, West cannot guard diamonds and clubs, nor East spades and diamonds, so the declarer makes the last three tricks and his contract.

16

THE GRAND COUP

PROBABLY the play which gives the greatest satisfaction to those who accomplish it successfully is the Grand Coup. It is one of the most spectacular plays seen at the bridge table but opportunities to use it are so rare that when they occur many players fail to recognize them. It is a trump reducing play by the declarer carried out to trap a defender whose high trumps cannot be led through in the normal way owing to the absence of trumps in the dummy hand. In order to avoid being compelled to lead trumps up to a defender, the declarer has to shorten his own trump suit by ruffing master cards in dummy. Here is an example in its simplest form :

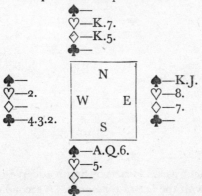

Spades are trumps and North leads the king of diamonds. When East follows suit, South must trump. If he discards the five of hearts he will have to take the next trick

with the six of trumps and lead from ace, queen to East's
king, knave, losing one trick. By trumping the king of
diamonds, even though it is a master card, he can put
North in with the king of hearts and the lead at the twelfth
trick will come through East's king, knave of spades up to
South's ace, queen.

In the early days of bridge the grand coup was considered so rare that to accomplish it was considered to be
a mark of distinction. Before long, however, it was put
in the shade by the repeated performance of the double
grand coup—getting rid of two trumps in order to produce the required end play. Today quite a number of
players can claim the distinction of having accomplished
a triple grand coup, getting rid of three trumps in order to
secure the required end play as in the following deal:

```
                    ♠—A.Q.7.
                    ♡—K.3.
                    ◇—K.Q.4.
                    ♣—A.Q.9.6.2.
     ┌─────────────────────────────────┐
♠—J.9.8.2.      │         N           │   ♠—10.4.3.
♡—            │                     │   ♡—Q.9.8.6.
◇—A.10.8.7.3.2. │   W         E       │   ◇—J.9.5.
♣—J.10.5.      │                     │   ♣—7.4.3.
                │         S           │
     └─────────────────────────────────┘
                    ♠—K.6.5.
                    ♡—A.J.10.7.5.4.2.
                    ◇—6.
                    ♣—K.8.
```

The contract was Six Hearts by South and West took the
first trick with the ace of diamonds. A second diamond
was taken by North's queen and South discarded the
five of spades. North led the king of hearts and when
West discarded a diamond the declarer could see that if

he had to lead trumps at the end up to East's queen, nine, he must lose a trick in the suit. The only possible chance to make his contract, therefore, lay in reducing his trumps to the same number as East, and leading from North's hand at the twelfth trick. The three of hearts was led to South's ten and the king of clubs was led and overtaken by the ace. The king of diamonds was ruffed by South and North was put in again, with the queen of clubs to lead the nine which South ruffed. The king of spades was led and overtaken by the ace so that North could lead another club which South ruffed. He had now reduced his trumps to the same number as East so that when North was put in with the queen of spades the lead at the twelfth trick came through East's queen, nine of spades up to South's ace, knave.

We have even heard from America of a Quadruple Grand Coup in which the declarer reduced his trumps by four by ruffing master cards in dummy. It is reproduced by Mr. G. S. Coffin in his standard book on End-plays.

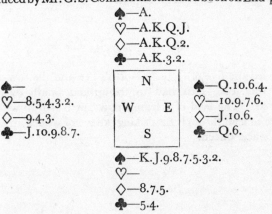

♠—A.
♡—A.K.Q.J.
♢—A.K.Q.2.
♣—A.K.3.2.

♠—
♡—8.5.4.3.2.
♢—9.4.3.
♣—J.10.9.8.7.

N
W   E
S

♠—Q.10.6.4.
♡—10.9.7.6.
♢—J.10.6.
♣—Q.6.

♠—K.J.9.8.7.5.3.2.
♡—
♢—8.7.5.
♣—5.4.

South bid Four Spades which North raised to Seven Spades and East doubled, West led the knave of clubs which was taken by North's king. The declarer then ruffed the ace, king, queen and knave of hearts, entered North's hand three times with ace, king, and queen of diamonds. The position now was :

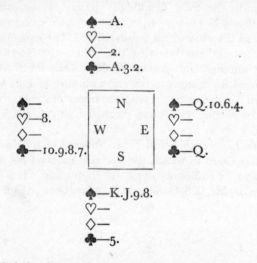

♠—A.
♡—
♢—2.
♣—A.3.2.

♠—
♡—8.
♢—
♣—10.9.8.7.

N
W   E
S

♠—Q.10.6.4.
♡—
♢—
♣—Q.

♠—K.J.9.8.
♡—
♢—
♣—5.

South led the five of clubs to North's ace and the two of clubs was led. East had to trump and South over-trumped. The lead of a trump now put North in with the ace to lead through East's king, knave of spades up to South's ace, queen.

17

DEFENSIVE PLAY

Good card play in defence is essential to success at bridge. It may be worth thousand of points in the course of a single evening. The declarer has a very definite advantage in planning his play through his knowledge of the cards in the partnership hands, while a defender has to work largely in the dark and to make a guess how he can help his partner to make the best use of the cards he holds. If he guesses correctly the contract can be defeated, if he does not, a contract which could have been defeated can be made. At rubber bridge where the cards are stacked in tricks the average player frequently overlooks the part played by the defenders, but at duplicate where each player keeps his cards to be replaced in the board and passed on to other tables there is more opportunity for study and careful examination, and a comparison of the results obtained presents an impressive picture of the value of accurate defensive play. The spectator watching a match between experts may see occasionally some very bad bridge but he will usually be impressed by the skill with which the defenders select the best line of play to make life difficult for the declarer.

Opening Leads

The most difficult moment for the defenders is frequently associated with the opening lead. This is a blind lead for, apart from the knowledge which he has

obtained from the bidding, the opener is in the dark
about the position and distribution of all the cards except
those in his own hand.   After he has led a card and
dummy's hand has been placed on the table much more
information is available.   The first thing to be considered
before making the blind opening lead is the contract in
which the hand is being played, whether it is with a trump
suit or in no trumps.   In a no trump contract long cards
in a suit have possible trick-taking value if they can be
established while he still retains an entry, but against a
trump contract they have little value, for it is almost
certain that they will be ruffed.   Against no trumps
therefore, the commonly accepted lead is the fourth
highest card of his longest suit.   This lead is disliked by
many experts because it gives away too much information
for by deducting the number of pips on the card led from
eleven both the partner and the declarer can calculate the
number of cards in the other three hands which are higher
than the card led.   If for example the distribution is :

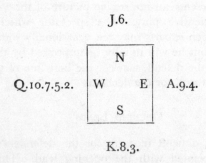

J.6.

Q.10.7.5.2.   W   E   A.9.4.

K.8.3.

On the lead of the five, East and South know that there are six cards higher than the five outside the leader's hand. There are two in dummy and two in each of the other hands and they can shape their play in the light of that information. Sometimes the knowledge of the distribution helps the declarer but more often it is useful to the defenders. Experts may possibly be able to find a better lead, but in the early days of bridge it is a safe lead. There are many who have been playing bridge for years who would find it difficult to explain why the value of the card led should be subtracted from eleven, but it is very simple. The lowest card in the pack is the two and the ace the highest card is the fourteenth. The card led is the five which normally would be deducted from fourteen, but as it is the fourth best card three of the higher cards must be in the leader's hand, reducing to eleven the number from which five must be subtracted to show the number of higher cards in the other three hands.

South is the declarer in a contract of Three No Trumps and West leads the six of hearts. Dummy puts down his hand in which the knave, eight and five of hearts can be seen. East holds the king, nine and four of hearts and by subtracting six, the value of the card led, from eleven he knows that the declarer can only hold one card which will beat the six, for there are only five cards which will do so and he and dummy hold two each. The declarer can almost certainly be placed with the ace or the queen. If East plays his king and the declarer holds the ace, dummy's knave will take a second trick in the suit. East will play the nine. If the declarer's card is the queen he will take the trick but there is nothing lost by holding up the king for the declarer must make one trick in the suit. If the declarer has the ace he will

F

probably hold it up, but East can safely lead the king to clear the suit so that his partner, if he has an entry, can make his long card or cards.

Top of Nothing Leads

There are occasions when it is obvious that the lead of the fourth highest card of the longest suit is not desirable. For example, the declarer in a contract of Three No Trumps has opened the bidding with One Spade and after a response of Two Hearts has bid Two Spades. When his partner has bid Three Clubs the opening bidder has bid Three No Trumps. The player whose duty it is to lead holds : ♠—K.J.9.4. ♡—10.7.4. ◇—Q.J.10 ♣—8.4.2. In these circumstances the lead of the four of spades, the fourth highest card of his longest suit would certainly present the declarer with at least one trick, for if, as is probable from the bidding, he holds five spades headed by the ace, queen, he must lose three tricks in the suit if he has to develop it himself. The obvious lead here is the queen of diamonds, the top card of a sequence. It can do no harm and if dummy should hold the king and his own partner the ace it can do quite a lot of good. If instead of holding the queen, knave, ten of diamonds his cards had been eight, seven, four, the best lead would have been the top card of one of the minor suits which would be recognized by his partner as a " top of nothing " lead. This " top of nothing " lead is chosen frequently when the opener has honour cards in the other suits. Sometimes with a short suit which has not been bid by either opponent the lead of the top card of that suit is effective, for it may assist the partner to develop his long suit, but it is not a lead which is recommended, for it is a shot in the dark and against no trumps it should not be made if a player has a long suit which may be established. No trump contracts frequently depend for their success or failure on whether the declarer or the defenders first establish the long cards in their suits and a player who fails to lead his long suit at once, and seeks instead a clever lead may find that he has surrendered his only chance of breaking the contract.

LEADS AGAINST NO TRUMPS

There are a number of recognized leads against no trump contracts which every player should know. With a suit of five cards headed by the ace, king, queen, the fourth highest card is led unless the hand contains a card of re-entry, in which case the king, queen, and ace are led out in the hope of dropping the outstanding cards. This is merely common sense. It is improbable that sound bidders will choose to play in a no trump contract with one suit unguarded and if the opener has no re-entry card, the lead of the three top honours will probably confine him to three tricks. If on the other hand he leads his fourth highest card and his partner has an entry card the return of the suit is likely to enable him to make four tricks. With six card suits headed by the ace, king, queen or seven card suits headed by the ace, king, the recommended lead is the ace followed by the king. The lead of an ace at no trumps, calls upon the partner to follow suit with his highest card. It is a very useful convention for the opening lead may be from A.K.J.10.7.4.3. On the lead of the ace, dummy plays the singleton two, and the next player with Q.8.5., dutifully plays the queen. The opener now knows exactly where he is and reels off his remaining six cards of the suit. Without this convention the partner would probably have played the eight, an encouraging card, but the opener would have switched to another suit fearing to set up a trick in the declarer's hand and hoping that his partner could get in to lead the suit up to him. Even if he continued with the king his partner's queen would block the suit on the third round. If there are six cards headed by the ace, king, the best lead is the fourth highest card unless the knave and ten are held also when the ace should be led, and if the queen does not fall the opener should switch to another suit in the hope that his partner will get in to lead the suit up to him. If his partner has a singleton this will throw away a trick but it will prevent the declarer from making a trick in the suit. With six cards, headed by the ace, queen, knave, ten or seven headed by the ace, queen, knave, the ace is the best lead if there is a re-entry card, but with no such card the queen should be led. When there is no very long suit, the fourth best card is usually the best unless there is a broken sequence. With A.K.J.10 or A.J.10.9. or K.J.10.9, lead the knave. With a sequence such as K.Q.J.9. or Q.J.10.6.5., the best lead is the highest card. Except when the king is led from ace, king, the lead of an honour card denies the possession of the next higher honour and shows a strong probability that the leader holds also the next lower honour. In leading, except from ace, king, it is the rule to select the higher of touching honours. The lead of a queen or a knave would tell the partner that the opener did not hold the card immediately higher in value than the card led. In following suit, the reverse is the rule, the lower of touching honours being played. The play of the knave for example would show that the player did not hold the ten but might possibly have the queen.

LEADS AGAINST SUIT CONTRACTS

Against a suit contract, entirely different considerations from those governing play at no trumps have to be employed. The value of long cards in a suit is greatly diminished, for they will probably be ruffed. The great object now is to make the best use of the good cards in the partnership hands which are possible winners. This does not mean that a player should be in a hurry to lead out his winners. Aces are useful, not only to make tricks but also to kill high honour cards in the declarer's hand, and to lead an ace, as some players do in order to look at dummy's cards while retaining the lead, may set up a king in the declarer's hand which could never take a trick if he had to lead the suit himself. The trick so presented to him may be the additional trick required to enable him to make his contract. With a five card suit headed by an ace, king, there is not the same objection to leading one of the top honours. There is little probability of making more than two tricks in the suit, the third round is certain to be ruffed, for one of the players will be unable to follow suit on the third round. The king should be led, followed by the ace. If the opener's partner has only two cards of the suit and can ruff the third round, he will signal for a continuance of the suit by playing his higher card followed by a lower card on the second round. If the only cards in a suit held are the ace and king, the ace is led first, followed by the king. Against a suit contract the lead of an ace does not call for the play of the partner's highest card, and the ace followed by the king is an intimation that the opener holds only two cards of the suit. The partner knows therefore that if he can get in to lead a third round before trumps are drawn, the opener will be able to ruff. This lead of the ace from ace, king only, is however not a good lead unless the opener has reason to believe that there is a quick entry to his partner's hand. If the opener's hand contains king, queen, knave of a suit, he should lead the king to set up at once two possible tricks. If he has four cards to the king, queen, ten, the king should be led, but this is not a particularly good lead, as, if dummy holds knave and two other cards and the declarer has the ace, both ace and knave will take tricks, whereas if the declarer has to develop the suit he will make only the ace.

With a hand which has no obvious opening lead, a player's choice may be in the nature of a gamble. He should however see what deductions can be drawn from the bidding. These may sometimes be very helpful. The opener may bid One Spade and receiving a response of Two Hearts he bids Three Clubs. The responder now says Four Clubs and the opener closes the bidding with Five Clubs. From the bidding it is obvious that neither opponent likes the major suit bid by his partner but both have good clubs. The player who has to make the opening lead holds : ♠—A.7.4. ♡—10.9.6. ◇—K.10.7.2. ♣—6.5.4. It appears likely that the declarer will have to make some of his tricks by cross ruffing and the best lead here may be a trump. The danger is that one of the opponents may have a long and solid major suit which can be run off as soon as trumps are drawn, but in that case the declarer would play out trumps himself.

If the partner has bid, the problem of the opening lead

is sometimes simplified. Not infrequently a player will intervene in the bidding, mainly in order to show his partner a safe opening lead. If the opener has a good suit of his own and his partner has bid another suit, the choice of which suit to lead is sometimes difficult. If the declarer is playing in a no trump contract, it is necessary to consider whether the opener's long suit or his partner's is likely to be established more easily and which hand is more likely to have a re-entry card to enable the long cards to be made. If it is decided to lead the partner's suit, which card should be led against a no trump contract. With only two cards of the suit the higher is the correct lead and with three small cards the highest is led. With three cards to an honour or four small cards the lowest card should be led unless there are touching honours when the higher should be led. If the partner's suit has been overbid on his right, for example when the bidding has been South One No Trump, North Two Diamonds, East Two Hearts, South Three Diamonds, North Three No Trumps it may be a good selection to lead an honour rather than the lowest card of the partner's suit. The declarer may sometimes be helped by this lead, but on the other hand it may be the one lead which will cause him to fail in his contract. Against a suit contract with four cards of the partner's suit headed by the ace, the ace is led, but with four cards headed by any other honour it is usual to lead a low card. With three cards headed by an honour there is no general rule. Some authorities recommend the lead of the honour, others prefer the lead of the lowest card.

With no guidance from the partner and a hand which contains no obvious opening level, it often pays to follow the old bridge maxim " through strength up to weakness. " This is particularly the case when dummy has shown a strong suit of his own and has been unable to support the suits bid by his partner. This was illustrated in the following deal in a match pointed duplicate pairs competition :

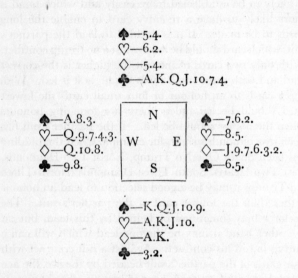

♠—5.4.
♡—6.2.
◇—5.4.
♣—A.K.Q.J.10.7.4.

♠—A.8.3.   ♠—7.6.2.
♡—Q.9.7.4.3.   ♡—8.5.
◇—Q.10.8.   ◇—J.9.7.6.3.2.
♣—9.8.   ♣—6.5.

♠—K.Q.J.10.9.
♡—A.K.J.10.
◇—A.K.
♣—3.2.

Both sides were vulnerable and South was the dealer. At nearly every table South became the declarer in a contract of Six Spades, though Six No Trumps would have been a better contract, as with match point scoring there is no premium for holding four or five honours in one hand. Most of the declarers made their contract, but one West player found the only defence to defeat it. He led the nine of clubs, the suit which North had bid persistently, deducing that North had long solid clubs and little else of value in his hand and hoping that by this lead he would break the declarer's line of communication with dummy. On taking the first trick a trump was led from North's hand. West took with the ace and led a second club. The declarer was now helpless for the long club suit was useless and he could not avoid losing a trick in hearts, and being one trick down. With any other opening lead but a club it was a simple matter to make twelve tricks.

The lead of a singleton against a suit contract is a very popular choice with average players. It can be a very good lead but it can also be a losing play. A singleton should never be selected merely because it is a singleton. With a strong trump holding, the lead of a singleton shows poor judgment for it may be much more profitable to retain trumps to kill those in the declarer's hand than to use them for ruffing. It may be far better for the declarer that the opening leader's trumps should be reduced by a ruff. With ace, ten and two other trumps, or queen, knave and one other, little or nothing may be gained by the lead of a singleton. Yet there are times when the lead of a singleton can be most effective. If the player with the opening lead has three trumps, headed by the ace or king and his partner has bid a suit which makes it likely that there is an immediate entry to his hand, it is better to open with a singleton rather than to lead the suit bid by the partner.

There are much the same objections to the lead of a doubleton as to the lead of a singleton and the prospect of obtaining a ruff is more remote. It can and not infrequently does prove a very good lead, but it should never be an automatic choice. It is difficult for the partner to distinguish between a doubleton and a singleton lead, and if he has the ace of the suit to decide whether he should or should not play it on the first round. When a doubleton is led and the partner has the ace and no re-entry card, he should duck the first round hoping that his partner can get in to lead the suit again when the ace will be played and another card of the suit led for a ruff. If it is a singleton however, the ace should be played at once and the suit returned for a ruff. If the doubleton is headed by an honour, the lead of the suit is not recommended unless it has been bid by the partner. The lead of the ace followed by a lower card will be successful if the partner holds the king, but the retention of the ace to kill a high card in the declarer's hand might be much better defensive play. When the defensive prospect appears to be hopeless, the lead of the king from king and another card may save the situation if the partner has the ace of the suit. The partners will congratulate themselves on clever play when this lead is successful, but it gives a very poor result if the declarer has ace and queen of the suit. Had it not been led the declarer would have finessed against it and the king would have made a trick. If the lead of the king gives the declarer his contract, the player who selects this opening lead is likely to receive anything but congratulations from his partner.

Opening leads against a slam contract in a suit are usually difficult. Some players automatically lead out an ace in the hope of making sure of at least one trick. Many slam contracts have been made by the declarer with the ace and king of one suit missing and this may be the one lead which will give the defenders two tricks, for the partner holding the king will call loudly for the continuance of the suit by playing a high card under the ace. But the lead of an ace against a slam contract is not regarded as a good lead. Most players have seen deals in which the ace has been trumped and the declarer has been left with two or three top cards in the suit on which he can obtain discards from the other hand. Any other lead might have made it more difficult to make the slam for the declarer would have had to use one of his high cards to draw the ace and thus would have reduced the number of discards from the other hand. Rather than lead out an ace it is better to attempt to build up a trick in one of the other side suits. South is the declarer in a contract of Six Spades and West holds ♠—7.3.2. ♡—A.10.9. ◇—Q.J.10. ♣—8.7.3.2. His best lead is the queen of diamonds. If his partner holds the king a possible trick is set up before the control of hearts has been surrendered. The declarer may have the ace and king of diamonds but even so no harm is done by leading the queen. If however, East has the king it will be possible to make it before diamonds can be discarded on one of the other suits. The full deal may have been :

♠—Q.9.8.6.
♡—6.
◇—9.4.3.
♣—A.K.10.9.2.

```
            N
♠—7.3.2.               ♠—5.4.
♡—A.10.9.2.    W   E   ♡—8.5.4.3.
◇—Q.J.10.              ◇—K.8.7.
♣—8.7.5.       S       ♣—Q.J.4.3.
```

♠—A.K.J.10.
♡—K.Q.J.7.
◇—A.6.5.2.
♣—6.

South is the declarer in a contract of Six Spades.
With these cards the lead of the ace of hearts would
present the declarer with his contract, for dummy could
discard two diamonds on the king and queen of hearts
and two diamonds could be ruffed.   Six tricks could be
made in spades, three in hearts, two in clubs and one in
diamonds.   But if the opening lead is the queen of diamonds the declarer must lose three tricks, for West will
get in with the ace of hearts and lead a diamond before
any discards can be made from dummy.   When leading
against a slam in a suit, therefore, it is advisable to
remember that the opportunities to play a winning card
which has had to be established by first drawing the
declarer's top card of the suit are limited, and that the
possible winner should be set up as soon as possible so

that it can be played before the declarer can obtain discards in the suit. Though an opening lead away from a king or queen may help the declarer, it may be the only lead which will set up the much needed second trick at once. The partner may have a card which will draw the declarer's guard in the suit. Though it is a lead which is made with extreme reluctance it may be the most effective lead against a suit slam. In choosing between a suit headed by a king and one headed by a queen, many good players prefer to lead away from the king for even if the declarer holds ace, queen of the suit there is still a possibility that the king will take a trick, whereas if the lead is away from a queen and the declarer takes the trick with the knave or ten the chance of the queen taking a trick is very remote.

Against a slam in no trumps, different considerations apply. There is no longer any risk that high cards will be ruffed and it is better to play a waiting game, than to attempt aggressive action. A high card may have a much better chance of taking a trick if the declarer has no indication which defender has it. Against a slam in no trumps it does not pay to be greedy. The main objective is to defeat the contract. By refraining from playing the card which would defeat the contract immediately, it may be possible to increase the penalty considerably, but it is always possible that there may be no other opportunity to play it. When this happens the offender must not expect to receive any sympathy from his partner. With A.K.J.7.5.2. of a suit the book lead may be the fourth highest card of the suit against the declarer playing in no trumps, but if the contract is Six No Trumps, the play of the two top honours will ensure that the points do not go to the declarer.

The choice of the opening lead is simplified if the contract is doubled by the opener's partner, or if a double of a suit bid which he has himself made for a take out is left in for a penalty. South, vulnerable, has dealt and bid One Spade. West holding ♠—9. ♡—A.Q.10.6. ◇—K.Q.8.4. ♣—Q.J.10.8., doubles for a take out. North passes and East decides to leave the double in. By so doing he has shown that he has a strong trump suit and has practically invited the opener to lead that suit. The full deal may be :

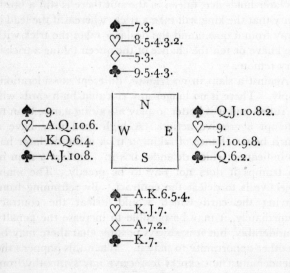

```
                 ♠—7.3.
                 ♡—8.5.4.3.2.
                 ◇—5.3.
                 ♣—9.5.4.3.

  ♠—9.              N           ♠—Q.J.10.8.2.
  ♡—A.Q.10.6.                   ♡—9.
  ◇—K.Q.6.4.      W   E         ◇—J.10.9.8.
  ♣—A.J.10.8.                   ♣—Q.6.2.
                    S

                 ♠—A.K.6.5.4.
                 ♡—K.J.7.
                 ◇—A.7.2.
                 ♣—K.7.
```

THE PETER

The play of an unnecessarily high card by the opener's partner is a definite encouragement to continue with the suit. The peter, the play of a high card followed by a lower card intimates that the opener's partner has control of the third round of the suit either because he holds the master card or because he can ruff. If against a suit contract the opening lead is the king, followed by the ace of the same suit and the opener's partner plays first the eight and then the four, the opener knows that his partner has either the queen or no more cards in the suit. It is a clear " come-on " signal and should not be made by a player simply because he has only two cards in the suit for he must also have at least one trump with which to ruff the third round.

Against a no trump contract the peter is used in a different way for it shows that the player employing it holds either two or four cards in the suit. It is a sound defensive play which is particularly useful when there is a long suit in dummy for which there is no re-entry card. If South is playing in a contract of Three No Trumps and North holds K.Q.J.10.4. of a suit, West with A.7.3. will play low when South leads the two to North's ten. The king will be led by North, East and South will follow and West is in difficulties. If he holds the ace up, North will have made two tricks and the second trick may give the declarer his contract, while if he plays the ace and South holds the missing card in the suit, four tricks in that suit will be set up in dummy. It is when dealing with a situation of this kind that the no trump peter is invaluable. West will recall that on the first round of the suit East played the six and on the second round the eight. He had not used the peter to show that he had four or two cards in the suit so he must have held originally three cards in the suit. It would be perfectly safe therefore to play the ace on the second round. If however East had played first the eight and then the six, West would hold up the ace for another round, knowing that South had the nine with which to put North in to make his long cards in the suit.

There is still another form of the high-low signal which can be useful in special circumstances. This is the trump peter or echo which can be employed when following suit as the declarer leads out trumps, its object being to inform the partner that he holds three trumps and hopes to use one for ruffing purposes. South is the declarer in Four Spades and West leads the king of hearts on which East plays the eight. The queen follows and East plays the two. South takes with the ace and leads out the ace and queen of trumps. West taking the second trump trick with the king may hesitate to lead a heart for East to ruff for fear that he may not have another trump. I the trump peter or echo is being used, however, there should be no doubt. With three trumps East would play high-low on the two rounds of trumps and West knowing that his partner had a trump left with which to ruff would lead another heart.

SUIT PREFERENCE SIGNALS

A defender can find quite a number of opportunities to give information to his partner. The discard of a high card a seven or higher, asks for that suit to be led. Even when there is no opportunity to call for a suit by a high discard it is possible both in leading and following suit to give useful guidance to the partner by suit preference signals. These signals can be invaluable, but they should be employed with caution, for their injudicious use can do much more harm than good. There are some players who appear to spend their time watching every card played to see if they cannot read it as a suit preference signal or who, if they find an ace in their hand, signal wildly to the partner to lead the suit so that they can get rid of it, possibly to the great satisfaction of the declarer. The suit preference signal is however a most useful device in its proper place, which is a position in which a change of suit is necessary, and the defender who has to lead has the choice of two suits. Here is an example, West leads against a contract of Four Spades by South :

♠—K.J.4.
♡—K.Q.J.7.6.
◇—K.J.
♣—K.J.6.

♠—9.8.6. ♡—A. ◇—10.8.7.5.2. ♣—5.4.3.2.	N W E S	♠—7.2. ♡—10.9.4.2. ◇—A.Q.6.3. ♣—10.9.8.

♠—A.Q.10.5.3.
♡—8.5.3.
◇—9.4.
♣—A.Q.7.

When West leads the ace of hearts East can see that it is probably a singleton and that hearts can be ruffed if he can secure the lead before the declarer can draw trumps. If after making the ace of hearts West leads a diamond, it is likely that two heart ruffs can be obtained but how can he tell him to lead a diamond. If the partners are playing the suit preference signal it is perfectly easy. On West's ace of hearts East plays the ten. This cannot be interpreted as an encouraging card asking for a continuance of the heart suit for there is obviously nothing to be gained by playing another heart. The play by East of a higher card than is necessary asks West to switch to the higher of the remaining suits outside hearts and trumps. Had East played a low heart under the ace he would have been asking for the lead of the lower ranking of the remaining suits. West having made his ace of hearts will lead a diamond, East will take the trick and will lead back a heart for a ruff. A second diamond lead will put East in again to enable the third round of hearts to be ruffed. East-West will therefore make five tricks, one in hearts, two in diamonds and two ruffs of hearts before the declarer can get in to draw trumps. If East had not been able to signal for a diamond lead, West after playing the ace of hearts would not have known whether to lead a diamond or a club. If he had chosen to lead a club, South would have got in at once, drawn trumps, and led out dummy's hearts on which he would have discarded the diamonds from his own hand and he would therefore have been able to make twelve tricks.

This suit preference signal can also be used by a player when leading. South is again the declarer in a contract of Four Spades, West holds ♠—9. ♡—A.K.7.3. ◇—A.Q.6.5. ♣—6.5.4.3. He leads the king of hearts and the declarer's partner puts down : ♠—A.K.10.6.3.2. ♡—8.6. ◇—7.2. ♣—J.10.8. The six of hearts is played from dummy and East plays the queen. The lead of the king of hearts is obviously a lead from ace, king, and East's play of the queen here, is an order to his partner to lead a small heart instead of the ace at the second trick. This is a recognized signal, which is very useful when a player holds queen, knave only of the suit of which his partner holds both ace and king, for it enables the partnership to win the second trick without losing control of the suit. It is also useful when as in this case the partner though having other cards in the suit can see from dummy's hand that a switch will be necessary after taking two tricks in hearts and there may be something to be gained by leading through the declarer's hand at the third trick. West is of course in thorough agreement and is anxious to tell East that when he takes the second trick he must lead a diamond. He does so by leading the nine of hearts. This being a higher card than is necessary can only be interpreted as a request for a lead of the higher of the remaining suits outside trumps. If a diamond is led he will make his ace and his queen, but if a club is led the declarer will make his contract.

There are players who do not like the suit preference signal because it does not always work out according to plan. In the last example given, if West had only ace, king, nine of hearts, his lead on the second round would still have been the nine which would have been interpreted as asking for a lead of a diamond, but his cards might have been : ♠—9. ♡—A.K.9. ◊—6.5.3.2. ♣—A.Q.6.5.4.

Some players would never dream of leading up to a tenace in dummy, but against a no trump contract it may be a very good lead. South is the declarer in a contract of Three No Trumps and West leads the six of spades. East plays the queen which is allowed to take the trick. Holding five clubs headed by the ace, queen and with king, knave, ten in dummy, the lead of a small club may be very much better than the immediate return of his partner's spade suit. When West gets in he should lead back clubs and East will make four tricks in the suit. This play will only fail if West had only a singleton club, and in that case the declarer can always make at least one trick in the suit. There are occasions when, playing against a trump suit, the declarer is presented with his contract because the defender's fight shy of a suit in which they could take three tricks, but one has ace, queen and another and the other has king, knave, ten. Neither is prepared to lead away from a tenace and the declarer is able to obtain discards before the suit is opened. While the lead away from a tenace is not recommended it should not be regarded as a lead which should not be made.

There are times when alert defence will make it possible to defeat the declarer by attacking him where he regards himself as the least vulnerable,—in the trump suit. Holding ace, knave only of trumps over the king, queen, when the declarer ruffs with the queen, a novice would probably over-ruff with the ace, failing to realize that if he is content to allow the queen to take the trick his own ace, knave will take two tricks while if he plays the ace the declarer will subsequently lead out the king and kill the knave. It is so obviously sound defence to refrain from playing the ace that it is surprising how many players do so without calculating the cost. It is much more difficult to visualize the possibility of making two tricks in trumps when holding only A.9.3., when sitting over a declarer holding K.Q.J.7.2., but it can be done. If West, holding A.K.Q.9.2. of a side suit makes the king and the ace, and finds that the remaining cards in the suit are in his hand and dummy's he will lead the two. His partner holding the ten of trumps and a small card will ruff with the ten. South will over-ruff with the knave, but must now lose two tricks in trumps to West's ace, nine, three.

18

DUPLICATE BRIDGE

DUPLICATE BRIDGE is the form of the game which offers the average player the best opportunity to test his or her skill and to learn by a comparison of results in what directions improvement in bidding and play are desirable. At duplicate bridge the same cards are played at a number of different tables. Instead of playing the cards into the centre of the table and gathering them in tricks the players play their cards on the table in front of them. When all four have played, each player retains his own card and places it face downwards on the table, the card pointing in the direction of the pair who have taken the trick. When all thirteen cards have been played the cards are collected and each player places his cards in a board with slots marked North, South, East and West and the board is passed to the next table. The score for tricks is the same as that for rubber bridge but 50 points are added for a part score bid and made, 300 points for a non-vulnerable game and 500 points for a vulnerable game.

Duplicate bridge contests can be arranged for teams of four, pairs or individuals. The usual number of boards played in a match between teams of four is 32. One pair from each team occupies the North-South positions at one table while the other pair play as East-West at the other. At the end of 16 boards, scores can be compared. The North-South pair at one table then change places with their other pair and play the East-West cards.

The team with the higher aggregate wins the match. The deal passes in rotation and in each 16 boards each player deals with the position, Love All, North-South Game, East-West Game, Game All.

In pairs competitions every North-South pair plays against every East-West pair, the number of boards varying with the number of pairs. As a rule the North-South pairs remain seated, while the East-West pairs move to the next higher numbered table and the boards move to the next lower numbered table. With an uneven number of tables this movement works smoothly, but with an even number of tables it would result in a pair being called upon to play for a second time, boards which they have already played. To avoid this breakdown of the movement a relay table is introduced between the two middle tables. If there are eight tables the relay table will be placed between tables four and five. If four boards are being played in each round the position of the boards when the first round starts will be Table 1, 1-4, Table 2, 5-8, Table 3, 9-12, Table 4, 13-16, Relay Table 17-20, Table 5, 21-24, Table 6, 25-28, Table 7, 29-32. There are now no boards left for Table 8, but throughout the competition Table 8 will share boards with Table 1. At the end of each round the North-South pair at Table 5 will place the boards they have played on the relay table, and the North-South pair at Table 4, will take the boards which have been out of play on the relay table. This Mitchell movement contest is the easiest to run and there is little chance of anything going wrong, for the North-South pairs receive their boards in consecutive order and any mistake in the movement of the boards would be noticed immediately. In this form of contest there are two winning pairs, one for the North-South and the other for the East-West section.

In individual contests or pairs competitions in which it is desired to find one absolute winner, a more complicated movement is necessary in order that all individuals or pairs shall play against each other, and they can no longer remain North-South or East-West throughout the session. In these conditions aggregate scoring would be no test and match point scoring is substituted, each pair scoring one match point on each board for every pair playing the same cards which returns a lower aggregate score. The movement of the pairs is so complicated that it is necessary to have a card on each table directing the pairs to their next position. Cards for movements of this kind can be purchased.

19

LAWS AND PROPRIETIES

THE perfect bridge player is always on guard against any
action or gesture which might possibly give him or her an
unfair advantage. There are few games at which it is
more easy to offend. Good manners and good temper
are essential. There is nothing more aggravating than
to sit at a table with a bad loser unless it is to have to
play with a gloating winner. The ideal player never
gives the slightest indication whether he is winning or
losing, whether he holds good or poor cards, whether he
approves or disapproves of a particular action taken by
any of the other players.

The game of bridge is regulated by definite laws and
proprieties which should be known to, and observed, by all
players. In framing these laws however it has been
assumed that bridge is a game which everyone will play
in a sporting spirit and with careful avoidance of any
action which may be calculated to give any player an
unfair advantage. Partners should inform their opponents what system they are playing. It is improper to
employ without explaining its meaning to the opponents,
a convention in calling or an unusual convention in play,
the significance of which may not be clear to them. It is
not an offence to depart from the system which is being
played. A player for example may make a bid or a
response without holding the strength required by the
system but if he does so it should deceive the partner as
well as the opponents. Private arrangements between

partners which result in actions which they both understand but are calculated to deceive the opponents are not
only unethical but may also be regarded as a form of
cheating. It is strictly unethical to play a card with
special emphasis or to hesitate unduly over the play of a
card when the play does not need consideration. The
man or woman who hesitates before playing a singleton
is guilty of conduct which is tantamount to cheating.

Players should guard against conduct which is involun-
tary, but which conveys a great deal of unfair information
to the partner. Some of this is entirely unconscious.
There are players who tell at once by their demeanour
when they have sorted their cards or by the inflexion of
their voices as they make their bids what kind of a hand
they hold. They are quite unaware that they do so and
even the most critical of their opponents would never
accuse them of giving unfair information deliberately to
their partners, but it imposes a handicap on the partner
who will be guilty of reprehensible conduct if he allows
his partner's hesitation, remark or manner to influence a
call, lead or play, though the opponents are perfectly
entitled, at their own risk, to draw any inferences they
like. Every bid should be made in the same tone of voice
and if possible without delay.

Both as declarer or as a defender a player should try to
anticipate the probable play of an opponent. A prolonged pause after a card has been played on his right
may be most enlightening to the opponents. They will
see that he has been faced by a problem which requires
consideration and will be able frequently to deduce the
nature of the problem and to plan their play to ensure the
best defence against it. The mere fact that a player
considers it necessary to hesitate before deciding which

card to play tells its own tale to an alert opponent.

It is an unfortunate feature of the game that it brings out the worst traits in some of the players. At other games players are quite satisfied to be handicapped according to their skill or lack of skill. At bridge there are many players who rate themselves far higher than they are entitled to do. If they hold good cards and win, they attribute it entirely to their own ability. If they lose, it is due to bad luck or more often to the alleged faults of their partners who are often far better players than they are. From the moment things begin to go wrong, players of this type begin to prepare their defence which consists largely of placing the blame for their own errors of bidding and play. When the hand has been played the attack on the partner opens and for the remainder of the rubber there is a feeling of irritation in the partnership which does not tend to produce the best results. We have all seen rubbers and matches lost through the quarrels of partners, an object lesson which should induce all players to endeavour to be good partners.

Another objectionable feature which should be avoided is double dummy criticism of an opponent. It is very easy after seeing all four hands to tell a declarer who has been one down that he could have made his contract by finessing a six at the second trick as the next player had the singleton five but it cuts no ice, for no player in his senses would be likely to do so.

The good player will endeavour to maintain good terms throughout the partnership. He will admit frankly his own mistakes but will gloss over those of his partner. Even after a bad crash he will try to soothe his partner, will urge that they should both forget it and will endeavour in subsequent deals to retrieve the ground which has been lost.

Every player should have a thorough knowledge of the Laws. Unfortunately a very large number of those who play regularly never take the trouble to acquire that knowledge, for they fail to realize that without it they are allowing themselves to play under a heavy handicap. Ignorance of the Laws also leads to quite unnecessary disputes, sometimes acrimonious, which may detract from the pleasure to be obtained from the game.

Before the Laws of Bridge were revised in 1948 there were a number of points of difficulty, but in the revision the wording has been made much more clear and difficulties of interpretation seldom arise now. It is advisable to have a copy of the Laws available when the game is being played so that when a point of difficulty arises it can be settled immediately.

Most of the disputes in the past have centred on two main points, improper calls and revokes. The most frequent improper call is a bid out of rotation. A bid out of rotation is usually the result of carelessness. With conversational bridge, or when there has been a prolonged inquest on the previous hands, a player anxious to get on with the game sometimes bids out of turn. When attention is called to the irregularity the call out of rotation is void and the auction reverts to the player whose turn it is to call. If a player has passed out of rotation before any player has bid or when it was the turn of the opponent on his right to call, the offender must pass when next it is his turn to call. If a player has made any call out of rotation other than a pass, the offender's partner must pass whenever it is his turn to call. If for example it is South's deal and West passes out of rotation the deal reverts to South, and whatever South bids West must pass for one round. If however instead of passing West has said, One Heart, the bid is void, the auction reverts to South and East is silenced for the duration of the auction. Whatever bid South makes West now has a very awkward problem to face. He knows that East must pass whenever it is his turn to bid and that if East-West hold the strong hands the opponents are not likely to keep the bidding open. If game is to be reached he must bid it at once and risk a heavy penalty if East is trickless.

The other improper call which most frequently causes trouble is the insufficient bid. This is more often the result of mis-hearing than of carelessness. Until 1948 the penalty for this offence was unduly severe, but with the revision of the Laws the offender has been allowed to substitute a sufficient bid or a pass. If he makes the lowest sufficient bid in the same denomination there is no penalty : if he makes any other bid his partner must pass whenever it is his turn to call : if he passes, his partner must pass whenever it is his turn to call and if the offending side become the defenders the declarer may require or forbid the opening lead of a specified suit.

The revoke, which is the play of a card of another suit when able to follow suit has probably led to many disputes at the bridge table. The Law has however now been greatly simplified. A revoke in any of the first eleven tricks becomes established when the offender or his partner leads or plays to a subsequent trick or signifies his intentions of doing so by naming a card by claiming or conceding a trick, or by exposing a hand. The penalty for a revoke is the transfer of two tricks to the non-offending side. These tricks must be won in play after the revoke. The revoke trick counts as a trick won in play after the revoke.   If there are no tricks won in play after the revoke there is no penalty.   If only one trick is won only one trick is transferred.

Some of the most acrimonious debates have arisen when to shorten the play the declarer has tabled his hand and claimed the remainder of the tricks.   A defender has challenged his claim and called on him to play out the hand.   Warned that he has miscalculated in some way the declarer has reviewed the play, come to the conclusion that he must have miscounted trumps and led the suit. One of the defenders plays a trump and the declarer's claim is then conceded.   To meet cases of this kind which gave the declarer an unfair advantage a new Law was introduced in 1948.   Now when the declarer makes a claim or concedes one or more of the remaining tricks he must face his cards on the table and make an adequate statement of his intended line of play.   A defender may then face his cards and suggest a play to his partner.   If either defender requires that play continues after the declarer's claim the declarer must play on and must make no play inconsistent with the statement he has made.   Unless he has stated his intention to do so at the time of making his claim he may not lead a trump while either defender has a trump and he may not finesse either in the suit led or in trumping the suit led.

Another of the new Laws with which players should be conversant, relates to improper remarks and gestures. This is a very difficult subject but our bridge legislators have endeavoured to deal with it.   They have included an omnibus clause providing penalties if by a remark or unmistakable gesture a player other than the declarer discloses his intentions or desires, or the nature of an unfaced hand, or improperly suggests a lead play or line of play, or improperly directs attention to the cards of a trick to which his partner has yet to play. If the offence occurred before the auction closed either opponent may require the offending side to pass whenever it is its turn to call, and if the offending side become defenders the declarer may require or forbid the opening lead of a specified suit. If the offence occurred after the auction closed, the declarer or either of the defenders may require the offender's partner to withdraw any lead or play which may have been suggested by the improper remarks or gesture. This penalty may be exacted on any trick subsequent to the offence, but only on one such trick.

ADVERTISING & PUBLICITY   ALGEBRA   AMATEUR ACTING   ANAT
BOOK-KEEPING   BRICKWORK   BRINGING UP CHILDREN   BUSINES
CHESS   CHINESE   COMMERCIAL ARITHMETIC   COMMERCIAL AR
COMPOSE MUSIC   CONSTRUCTIONAL DETAILS   CONTRACT BRIDGE
SPEEDWORDS   ECONOMIC GEOGRAPHY   ECONOMICS   ELECTR
ENGLISH GRAMMAR   LITERARY APPRECIATION   ENGLISH RENASCE
REVIVAL   VICTORIAN AGE   CONTEMPORARY LITERATURE   ETCHIN
FREELANCE WRITING   FRENCH   FRENCH DICTIONARY   FRENCH
LIVING THINGS   GEOLOGY   GEOMETRY   GERMAN   GOOD
GOOD CONTROL OF INSECT PESTS   GOOD CONTROL OF PLANT DISEA
GOOD FARMING BY MACHINE   GOOD FARM WORKMANSHIP   GOO
GOOD MARKET GARDENING   GOOD MILK FARMING   GOOD PIG KEE
GOOD ENGLISH   GREEK   GREGG SHORTHAND   GUIDEBOOK TO TH
GREAT   BOLIVAR   BOTHA   CATHERINE THE GREAT   CHATHAM   CLEM
LIBERALISM   HENRY V   JOAN OF ARC   JOHN WYCLIFFE   LENIN   LOUIS
ROBES   HASTINGS
HOUS   REPAIRS
WRIT   ᏀIVE INSTRUCTION   ND TOO
MECH   LCRAFT
MOTO   TO A WISE MAN···   FICIENCY
PHYSI   DESIGN
ADMI   NG   RE
PHR   OOK   SAILING   SALESMANSHIP   SECRETA   ACTICE
DEBATE   SPELLING   STAMP COLLECTING   STUDE   DE   ST
TYPEWRITING   USE OF GEOGRAPHY   WAY TO POETR   WRIT
COOKERY FOR GIRLS   DOGS AS PETS FOR BOYS AND GIRLS   KNIT
PHOTOGRAPHY FOR BOYS AND GIRLS   RADIO FOR BOYS   RIDING F
SOCCER FOR BOYS   STAMP COLLECTING FOR BOYS AND GIRLS   WO
ACTING   ANATOMY   ARABIC   ASTRONOMY   BANKING   BEE
CHILDREN   BUSINESS ORGANISATION   CALCULUS   CANASTA   C
COMMERCIAL ART   COMMERCIAL CORRESPONDENCE   COMMERC
CONTRACT BRIDGE   COOKING   CRICKET   DRAWING   DRESSI
ECONOMICS   ELECTRICITY   ELECTRICITY IN THE HOUSE   ELOCUT
ENGLISH RENASCENCE   ENGLISH RENASCENCE TO THE ROMANTIC
LITERATURE   ETCHING   EVERYDAY FRENCH   TO EXPRESS YOURS
DICTIONARY   FRENCH PHRASE BOOK   GARDENING   GAS IN TH
GERMAN   GERMAN DICTIONARY   GERMAN GRAMMAR   GERMAN
CONTROL OF PLANT DISEASES   GOOD FARM ACCOUNTING   GO
GOOD FARM WORKMANSHIP   GOOD FRUIT FARMING   GOOD GRA
GOOD MILK FARMING   GOOD PIG KEEPING   GOOD POULTRY KEE
GREGG SHORTHAND   GUIDEBOOK TO THE BIBLE   HINDUSTANI
CATHERINE THE GREAT   CHATHAM   CLEMENCEAU   CONSTANTINE COC
ARC   JOHN WYCLIFFE   LENIN   LOUIS XIV   MILTON   PERICLES   PETER TH
USE OF HISTORY   WARREN HASTINGS   WOODROW WILSON   HOCKE
HOUSEHOLD ELECTRICITY   HOUSE REPAIRS   ITALIAN   JOINERY
MANAGEMENT   MATHEMATICS   HAND TOOLS   ENGINEERING
DRAUGHTSMANSHIP   METEOROLOGY   MODELCRAFT   MODERN DAN
MUSIC   NORWEGIAN   PERSONAL EFFICIENCY   PHILOSOPHY   PHOT
SHORTHAND   PLANNING AND DESIGN   PLUMBING   POLISH   POR